BLOOD IN THE TRACKS

Also Published by the University of Minnesota Press

Blue Guitar Highway
by Paul Metsa

Cosmic Trip: Rock Concerts at the Minneapolis Labor Temple, 1969–1970
by Christian A. Peterson

Everybody's Heard about the Bird:
The True Story of 1960s Rock 'n' Roll in Minnesota
by Rick Shefchik

BLOOD IN THE TRACKS

THE MINNESOTA MUSICIANS
BEHIND DYLAN'S MASTERPIECE

Paul Metsa and Rick Shefchik

UNIVERSITY OF MINNESOTA PRESS
MINNEAPOLIS
LONDON

Published by the University of Minnesota Press
111 Third Avenue South, Suite 290
Minneapolis, MN 55401-2520
http://www.upress.umn.edu

ISBN 978-1-5179-1427-1 (hc)
ISBN 978-1-5179-1720-3 (pb)

Library of Congress record available at https://lccn.loc.gov/2023001501.

Printed in the United States of America on acid-free paper

The University of Minnesota is an equal-opportunity educator and employer.

30 29 28 27 26 25 24 23   10 9 8 7 6 5 4 3 2 1

This book is dedicated to Peter Ostroushko and Chris Weber,
who gave their lives to music

Contents

Introduction

WHEN SOMETHING IS RIGHT

FOR DECADES, A BOOTLEG CD TITLED *BLOOD ON THE TRACKS:* *The New York Sessions* circulated among Bob Dylan's most devoted fans, and it became close to gospel among this cognoscenti that the released version of Dylan's masterpiece (half of which was recut in a Minneapolis studio) was in fact an inferior makeover of an album that was nearly perfect in its original form. This opinion held that Dylan had lost his nerve on the eve of the release of a record that was vitally important to his career; that he mistakenly listened to his provincial brother, David Zimmerman, who convinced him the songs were too dark, too stark, too mellow for the album to become a hit; and that instead of trusting the work and instincts of famous New York engineer Phil Ramone and the experienced studio pros who contributed their chops to the original recordings, he instead relied on an anonymous group of pickup musicians in Minneapolis, who weren't worthy of the responsibility, to re-record five of the ten tracks on the album.

Among Dylan's peers who preferred the original New York version of the album were Robbie Robertson ("The first recordings he played for me still stuck in my mind") and Joni Mitchell ("They butchered it"). When such heavyweights express their preference, the rest of the music world tends to fall in line. Even rock critic Robert Christgau, who gave the album a rare A in his monthly *Village Voice* Consumer Guide, referred to the "unknown Minneapolis studio musicians who impose nothing beyond a certain anonymous brightness." Yet it was that "anonymous brightness" that may well have elevated *Blood on the Tracks* from great to a masterpiece. Surely there isn't much room for improvement when an album is ranked by *Rolling Stone* as the ninth best ever recorded, as of 2020.

For forty-four years, the Minneapolis pros who played on the revised songs on *Blood on the Tracks* went uncredited. Because Dylan delivered the re-recorded tracks to Columbia just weeks ahead of the album's scheduled January 1975 release, the label chose not to alter the already printed back-cover credits—which only mentioned the New York studio musicians who accompanied Dylan on the original recordings, laid down in September 1974. The Minneapolis musicians who recut five of the album's ten songs with Dylan that December were told that their names would appear on the album's credits if and when there was a second pressing. The album was an immediate success, quickly selling out the initial run of 150,000 copies, but Columbia did not alter the credits on the second pressing or any subsequent editions. Indeed, if you are still of a mind to purchase the currently available—and remastered—CD version of *Blood on the Tracks*, you will find the credits read exactly as they did when the album was first released.

Fortunately, Dylan began a comprehensive archival release program several decades ago, making commercially available the outtakes and concert recordings that had made him the most extensively bootlegged artist in music history. In 2018, Dylan and Columbia finally got around to releasing *More Blood, More Tracks*, a six-CD collection that included every existing outtake and officially released version of each of the songs recorded during the *Blood on the Tracks* sessions in New York and Minneapolis. On that collection the Minneapolis musicians (drummer Bill Berg, bassist Billy Peterson, keyboardist Gregg Inhofer, guitar players Kevin Odegard and Chris Weber, and mandolin player Peter Ostroushko) received their first official credits for their work on the album. Fans of the album and Dylan scholars were finally able to listen to all versions of the songs and decide for themselves whether Dylan had made a mistake recutting five of the songs, as both the New York and Minneapolis studio versions could now be heard. It was the culmination of a long march to redemption for a group of unjustly ignored but richly deserving Minnesota musicians.

While one opinion has always held that the New York musicians (Eric Weissberg, Tom McFaul, Tony Brown, Charles Brown III, Richard Crooks, Buddy Cage, and Paul Griffin) were seasoned pros with far more impressive credentials than their Minneapolis counterparts, history has shown that the band assembled by David Zimmerman at Sound 80 had every bit the experience, résumé, and range as the New York musicians. As their life stories unfold in this book, it will become clear that these musicians were supremely qualified to make their vital contributions to Dylan's masterpiece. In addition, there is evidence to suggest that Sound 80 engineer Paul Martinson—not having worked with Paul Simon, Barbra Streisand, or Frank Sinatra, as had Phil Ramone—was equally skilled at twisting the knobs, catching the best performances, and, just as important, providing the right tone and atmosphere to bring out the best in a mercurial figure like Bob Dylan.

Perhaps most central to the successful midcourse correction that resulted in the final version of *Blood on the Tracks* is that those five re-recorded songs were performed by Dylan with musicians who shared his Minnesota DNA. Every note played on the Minneapolis sessions was executed by players who had come of age in the land of 10,000 lakes, 67,000 farms, and 220,000 snowmobiles. They had never taken their careers for granted; rather, they cherished their places in the music world that often thought of them as somehow second-class. These performances reflected hard-earned musical savvy strained through the experience of hundreds of gigs in far north bars, dance clubs, coffeehouses, and juke joints—just the kinds of places Dylan grew up playing in and singing about. The compatibility was palpable, and the results speak for themselves.

This is not a book solely about Bob Dylan. It's a book about the inspiration, creation, and sustained life span of one of the enduring masterpieces of American recorded music. It's a book about the many lives that contributed to that masterpiece, including but not limited to that of the Minnesota bard himself. And it is a book that gives long overdue credit to the musical magic that took place at Sound 80 Studios in Minneapolis in late December 1974. On "You're Going to Make Me

Lonesome When You Go," perhaps the most covered song from *Blood on the Tracks*, Dylan famously sang, "When something's not right, it's wrong." Conversely, when something is right, it should be acknowledged, examined, and celebrated. This book is that acknowledgment, examination, and celebration.

I
"Heading Out for the East Coast"

FIFTEEN YEARS AFTER LEAVING HIS HOMETOWN OF HIBBING, Minnesota, as a complete unknown, Bob Dylan had become by 1974 perhaps the most influential and intensely scrutinized musician in popular music. The world had become used to anticipating what Bob Dylan would do next. He was so ubiquitous that the most famous rock stars were name-checking him in songs: Simon and Garfunkel in "A Simple Desultory Philippic" (1966), the Beatles in "Yer Blues" (1968), The Who in "The Seeker" (1970), David Bowie in "Song for Bob Dylan" (1971), Rick Nelson in "Garden Party" (1972), and Roger McGuinn of the Byrds in "I'm So Restless" (1973).

And yet his marriage was unraveling and his career was at a perilous crossroads. It should have been the culmination of everything he had dreamed of. His high school yearbook stated that his goal was to join Little Richard's band. His high school girlfriend, Echo Helstrom, told reporter Toby Thompson of the *Village Voice* in 1969: "We'd talk about getting married a lot, just to get out of Hibbing for one thing, but Bob always said no, we can't even think about that. Would interfere with our careers. It was always the career with Bob. I thought about a career a lot too, sure, but with Bob it was an obsession. He really wanted to show everybody. And he has, I guess. Though few people in Hibbing could even care."

Those who knew him from his earliest days as a folk singer in New York City recognized that there was something special, a certain kind of genius, about him. "Dylan's mind seemed to make strange jumps, like electricity," fellow folk singer Eric von Schmidt told biographer Anthony Scaduto. "His mind was the most exciting . . . like a calypso mind, making instantaneous sorts of connections, relating seemingly unrelated things and putting them together into something marvelous."

"He had the vision and the talent to expand a pop song until it contained the whole world," Bruce Springsteen said at Dylan's induction into the Rock & Roll Hall of Fame. "He invented a new way a pop singer could sound. He broke through the limitations of what a recording artist could achieve, and he changed the face of rock and roll forever and ever." After establishing himself as an important topical songwriter, Dylan had burst into the national consciousness with a series of dizzyingly imaginative songs and albums ("Like a Rolling Stone," *Blonde on Blonde*, and so on) that had propelled him to the top of the pop charts and led the media to declare him the "voice of his generation." Rock critic Greil Marcus wrote that in 1965 Dylan "held a stage that no one has more than mounted since—a stage that may no longer exist. . . . Bob Dylan seemed less to occupy a turning point in popular space and time than to be that turning point."

It was too much.

"The big bugs in the press kept promoting me as the mouthpiece, spokesman, or even conscience of a generation," Dylan wrote in his *Chronicles, Volume One*, his memoir published in 2004. "That was funny. All I'd ever done was sing songs that were dead straight and expressed powerful new realities. I had very little in common with and knew even less about a generation that I was supposed to be the voice of."

Trying to deal with the pressure and meet the expectations of being an international rock star had culminated in a drug-fueled, controversy-laden tour of Europe in the spring of 1966, followed by a motorcycle accident near his home in Woodstock, New York. He suffered fractured vertebrae and recovered fairly quickly, but he took the accident as a signal that his life was out of control. What mattered most to him now was his wife, Sara Lownds, whom he had married in late 1965, and his growing family. He ceased touring, did not release an album for a year and a half, and essentially dropped out of sight. Keeping up with current events and maintaining a career in the media spotlight were no longer important to him. "I was determined to put myself beyond the reach of it all," he wrote in *Chronicles*. "I was a family man now, didn't want to be in that group portrait."

The music he did make during this period was a dramatic change from the long, impassioned, imagery-rich, and allegorical treatises for which he'd become famous. Instead, he gathered with members of The Band, his touring group, and made home recordings of dozens of reflective, whimsical, and mysterious ditties drawn from the old-time American traditions of pop, folk, country, and blues. He sent the songs to his publisher as demos but did not release them himself. In late 1967 he released *John Wesley Harding*, a brief album rife with simple melodies and religious symbolism. He did not tour to support the album, but his efforts to avoid the public spotlight were only partially successful.

He had moved to Woodstock in 1964 to escape the magnifying glass that New York City had become for him, but now rogue hippies, radicals, moochers, demagogues, drifters, dropouts, druggies, and worshippers had begun flocking to his upstate home, to the point where he felt it was necessary to arm himself with a pair of pistols and a Winchester rifle.

Riding in the car one day, Robbie Robertson of The Band asked him, "Where do you think you're gonna take it?"

"Take what?" he asked.

"The whole music scene."

"The whole music scene!" he replied, recounting the incident in *Chronicles*. "It was like dealing with a conspiracy. No place was far enough away. I don't know what everybody else was fantasizing about but what I was fantasizing about was a nine-to-five existence, a house on a tree-lined block with a white picket fence, pink roses in the backyard. Woodstock had turned into a nightmare, a place of chaos. Now it was time to scramble out of there in search of some new silver lining and that's what we did."

In an admitted effort to totally remake his image, Dylan went to Nashville in 1969 and recorded an album of pleasant, mostly original country music—perhaps the most unlikely direction his passionate fans could have expected. So much the better, as far as Dylan was concerned. He "made sure it sounded pretty bridled and housebroken," he wrote in *Chronicles*. "The music press didn't know what to make of it. . . . People scratched their heads. . . . Sometime in the past I had written and performed songs that were most original and most influential, and I didn't know if I ever would again and I didn't care." In case anyone was still expecting Dylan to jump back into the rock 'n' roll whirlwind he'd been riding in the mid-'60s, he followed up *Nashville Skyline* with the 1970s' *Self Portrait*, a puzzling collection of tepid leftovers and listless cover songs. The album's review on the website AllMusic.com states, "There has never been a clearer attempt to shed an audience." More bluntly, *Rolling Stone* reviewer Greil Marcus began his review with, "What is this shit?"

He moved his family back to New York City, hoping his sagging sales and tattered reputation as a trailblazer would allow him to sink into some sort of anonymity. But he'd created too many followers to disappear that easily. A self-proclaimed Dylanologist named A. J. Weberman found out where he lived and went through his garbage every night, looking for clues to Dylan's new direction. His next album, *New Morning* (1970), hinted at a return to more topical rock 'n' roll, but it was mostly a collection of safe, personal observations about his own life. "Message songs?" he wrote in *Chronicles*, looking back on the reaction to *New Morning*. "There weren't any. Anybody listening for them would have to be disappointed. As if I was going to make a career out of that anyway. Regardless, you could still feel the anticipation in the air. When will the old him be back? When will the door burst open and the goose appear? Not today."

And still his old friends and fans refused to give up hope. In 1972, his former duet partner Joan Baez, who had never strayed far from the protest songs of yore, called him out with a song called "To Bobby," which included the lyrics, "Do you hear the voices in the night, Bobby? They're crying for you. See the children in the morning light? Bobby, they're dying."

While Dylan dismissed such pleas ("I was not a spokesman for anything or anybody. . . . I was only a musician"), he did seem to be missing the attention he once commanded. He took a role in Sam Peckinpah's

1973 Western film *Pat Garrett & Billy the Kid* and wrote and recorded the film's soundtrack album. The song "Knockin' on Heaven's Door" became a surprise hit, reaching number 12 on the Billboard singles chart. As Dylan's interest in the entertainment business seemed to be increasing, so did the entertainment business's interest in him. He left Columbia after a dozen years, wooed away by David Geffen's Asylum label, known for its roster of West Coast artists, including Joni Mitchell, Jackson Browne, and the Eagles.

Suddenly, he was back in the game. The 1974 studio album he recorded with The Band, *Planet Waves*, was the first number-one album of his career. It also sent out signals that his personal life was not as contented as the bland lyrics on *Nashville Skyline* and *New Morning* had suggested. On the song "Going, Going, Gone," he sang, "I been hangin' on threads, I been playin' it straight. Now, I've just got to cut loose before it gets late. So I'm going, I'm going, I'm gone." On "Tough Mama" he sounded positively morose: "I'm crestfallen, the world of illusion is at my door. I ain't a-haulin' any of my lambs to the marketplace anymore. The prison walls are crumblin', there is no end in sight. I've gained some recognition, but I lost my appetite." Only the seemingly devotional "Wedding Song" appeared to sustain his claim that his marriage and family were more important to him than his career and his image: "It's never been my duty to remake the world at large, nor is it my intention to sound a battle charge, 'cause I love you more than all of that with a love that doesn't bend, and if there is eternity I'd love you there again."

The subsequent tour—his first since 1966—produced another successful album, the live *Before the Flood*, which peaked at number 3. But the *Planet Waves* tour also reintroduced Dylan to the pleasures and perils of rock 'n' roll on the road—a perpetual bacchanal that had driven him into seclusion eight years earlier. This time, according to several of his fellow musicians, Dylan was not always successful at resisting the usual temptations. The strain showed on his marriage; when the tour ended, rather than going home to his family and new house in Malibu, he first went to New York City, where he enrolled in a painting class taught by Norman Raeben, who did not know or care who Dylan was. Raeben taught him to "put my mind and my hand and my eye together

Bob Dylan in 1974, at work on *Blood on the Tracks*. Photograph by Barry Feinstein.

in a way that allowed me to do consciously what I unconsciously felt," Dylan told *Rolling Stone* reporter Jonathan Cott in 1978. "And I didn't know how to pull it off. I wasn't sure it could be done in songs because I'd never written a song like that. But when I started doing it, the first album I made was *Blood on the Tracks*."

Dylan had been searching for a way to start writing songs "unconsciously" again—the way he had in the mid-1960s. "Right through the time of *Blonde on Blonde* I was doing it unconsciously," he told Cott. "Then one day I was half-stepping, and the lights went out. And since that point, I more or less had amnesia." The classes with Raeben woke him up, and his notebooks began to fill with song lyrics. Unfortunately, the classes also drove him further away from Sara.

"I went home after that and my wife never did understand me ever since that day," he told Peter Oppel of the *Dallas Morning News* in 1978. "That's when our marriage started breaking up. She never knew what I was talking about, what I was thinking about. And I couldn't possibly explain it." One thing he was thinking about was his relationship with Ellen Bernstein, a Columbia publicist he had met in California during the *Planet Waves* tour. He had spent time with her at her home in Mill Valley earlier in 1974, and then he invited her to join him that summer at the farm he owned northwest of Minneapolis.

It was a time of enormous creativity for Dylan, who wrote more than a dozen songs during that period, most of them meditations on personal relationships, a topic he'd written about only obliquely since his 1964 album *Another Side of Bob Dylan*, which included the eight-minute "Ballad in Plain D," a song that described the breakup of his relationship with girlfriend Suze Rotolo in harrowing detail. He had since expressed regret for airing that much of his private life in public, and his few subsequent relationship songs were carefully devoid of specifics.

But now, feelings of both love and regret were pouring out of him, as his classes with Raeben had given him a new way to express himself. The songs that would become *Blood on the Tracks* were mostly written on a Martin 00-18 guitar in open D tuning, which he'd sporadically used as a young folk singer, on such songs as "Tomorrow Is a Long Time," "Walkin' Down the Line," and "Oxford Town." Now he'd returned to the tuning for its folkier sound, and it could not be a coincidence that he admitted to an obsession with *Blue,* the classic 1971 album by Joni Mitchell, who used open tunings exclusively on her guitar-based songs. While visiting Bernstein in Mill Valley, that guitar, a gift from singer-songwriter David Bromberg, was stolen out of his van. He spent much of the rest of the year searching for a replacement. That summer and fall, he played a Martin 00-21, a slot-head twelve-fret model from the 1950s.

The lyrics for the songs he wrote that spring and summer were all scrawled in three 5-by-3-inch spiral notebooks that cost the world-famous songwriter just nineteen cents apiece. They included:

"Lily, Rosemary and the Jack of Hearts," a sprawling, nine-minute shaggy-dog tale about a cabaret singer, a rich man and his jealous wife, and a smooth, mysterious stranger who was engineering a bank robbery.

"Tangled Up in Blue," the most famous and enduring song of the batch, which seems to tell the story of Dylan's early years as a traveling musician, his first love, their breakup, and his subsequent endeavors—told in both shifting chronology and point of view, as influenced by Raeben's teachings.

"Shelter from the Storm," an ode to a woman who offers a battered man succor but then turns him out again.

"If You See Her, Say Hello," a tender ballad of regret, looking back on a relationship that failed and expressing dim hope it might be revived.

"Simple Twist of Fate," another reminiscence of an old love affair, initially subtitled "4th Street Affair," perhaps after the street where Dylan lived with Suze Rotolo.

"Idiot Wind," in its initial version an acoustic-based expression of dismay and bewilderment at the behavior of a loved one, while allowing for the possibility that the problems were not all one-sided.

"You're Gonna Make Me Lonesome When You Go," an upbeat, melodic folk song professing love for a departing companion, generally thought to be Ellen Bernstein because of lyrical references to the cities where she was born and later lived.

"You're a Big Girl Now," the album's most forlorn breakup song, in which the singer describes his pain like a corkscrew to his heart but swears he can change.

"Meet Me in the Morning," a basic blues song lamenting the loss of a woman who treated him unkindly and then left him.

"Buckets of Rain," a snappy acoustic-based riff that exudes lust for a tantalizing lover.

He was considering two other songs: "Up to Me," which basically shared a melody with "Shelter from the Storm" and was eventually covered by Roger McGuinn on his 1976 album *Cardiff Rose*; and "Call Letter Blues," a variation of "Meet Me in the Morning." The notebook also contained lyrics for several songs that to date have never surfaced with melodies: "There Ain't Gonna Be Any Next Time," "Belltower Blues," "Church Bell Blues," "Where Do You Turn (Turning Point)," "It's Breakin' Me Up," "Don't Want No Married Woman," and "Ain't It Funny."

He began playing the songs for friends and fellow musicians in California and Minnesota. Stephen Stills and bassist Tim Drummond were the recipients of a recital in a St. Paul hotel room that summer; Stills later was critical of Dylan's musicianship, but Drummond raved about the quality of the songs. A more telling audition occurred at the San Francisco apartment of Mike Bloomfield, the former Paul Butterfield Blues Band lead guitarist who made such an important contribution to Dylan's first electric performances and recordings in 1965. Bloomfield was eager to record with Dylan again but had difficulty playing along as Dylan performed his new songs one after another. Bloomfield described the experience to Larry "Ratso" Sloman in 1975, for Sloman's book *On the Road with Bob Dylan*:

He took out his guitar, he tuned to open D tuning and he started playing the songs non-stop. . . . He just played them all and I just sorta picked along. . . . Any attempt I made to say, "Hey Bob, stop! Do it from the beginning so I [can] learn it," or, "Let me write a chart up, play it for me just verse and chorus" [was ignored]. But see, he was selling the whole song, and they weren't short songs. He was singing the whole thing and I was saying, "No man, don't sing the whole thing, just sing one chorus and if it's not gonna change let me write it down, so I can play it with you." He didn't. He just kept on playing . . . one after another and I got lost. They all began to sound the same to me. They were all in the same key, they were all long. I don't know, it was one of the strangest experiences of my life. And it really hurt. . . . He was sort of pissed that I didn't pick it up.

But Dylan was determined to present his new batch of songs in a softer, more singer-songwriter style, and if that meant old rock pals like Bloomfield couldn't fit in, so be it. James Taylor, Paul Simon, Joni Mitchell, Neil Young, John Denver, Gordon Lightfoot, and Cat Stevens were all selling millions of albums and getting constant radio airplay, and Dylan certainly knew that he had paved the way for each of them. Despite the initial success of *Planet Waves* and *Before the Flood*, Dylan was disappointed at Asylum's failure to generate a hit single from either album ("On a Night Like This" peaked at only 44 on the Billboard singles chart); both albums fell off the charts relatively quickly. By the summer of 1974, he was considering re-signing with Columbia. The brief trip up the charts he'd experienced with Asylum seemed to generate a desire for something greater—something more akin to the heady days when "Like a Rolling Stone" and "Rainy Day Women #12 & 35" saturated the airwaves a decade earlier.

The twin instincts of getting back on the charts and baring his troubled soul created the backdrop for the recording of *Blood on the Tracks*. Dylan has repeatedly denied that this is his "divorce album," claiming in *Chronicles, Volume One* that the entire album was "based on Chekhov short stories—critics thought it was autobiographical—that was fine." Yet syndicated gossip columnist Earl Wilson reported on June 22, 1974, that "Bob Dylan and wife Sara (parents of five) [have] separated. He is friendly with Laurie [misspelling of Lorey] Sebastian, ex-wife of John Sebastian of the Lovin' Spoonful." Lorey Sebastian issued a flat denial, but Dylan's response was to sign a new contract with Columbia and record his emotionally charged songs for a new album.

On Monday, September 16, 1974 (Rosh Hashanah, Jewish New Year), Dylan commenced recording at A&R Recording Studios in New York City, the former Columbia Records Studio A where Dylan had recorded his first six albums in the 1960s and his signature song "Like a Rolling Stone." Studio A1 was located on the seventh floor of 799 Seventh Avenue in Manhattan, a boxlike building with a peaked copper roof to block electrical interference. This 65 x 55-foot room with a 40-foot ceiling had belonged to Columbia since the 1930s, until they sold it to recording engineer Phil Ramone in 1968. At that point it became A&R Studios.

Ramone, who died in 2013, started A&R Studios with Jack Arnold in 1958 at 112 West Forty-eighth Street. In his 2007 autobiography, *Making Records*, Ramone wrote, "Our reputation as a jingle house grew through word of mouth, and the big Madison Avenue ad agencies became our best daytime clients." Soon they began making pop records, beginning in 1958 with *The Genius of Ray Charles*. Ramone engineered many hits for Dionne Warwick, and the landmark bossa nova album by Stan Getz and João Gilberto was recorded there in 1963. He engineered the mixing session for Lesley Gore's "It's My Party" and worked on many of her subsequent hits. After a temporary move to a smaller studio in 1968, Ramone and Arnold bought the flagship Columbia Records Studio A1. The albums recorded in Studio A1 included Van Morrison's *Moondance*; Elton John's first American concert broadcast, *11-17-70*; Paul Simon's *Still Crazy After All These Years*; Billy Joel's *The Stranger*, *52nd Street*, *Glass Houses*, and *The Nylon Curtain*; and Frank Sinatra's *L.A. Is My Lady*, the last recording made there before the building was razed in 1984.

The studio represented both a return to past glories and a fresh start for Dylan. Even his original champion at Columbia Records, legendary producer John Hammond, was there the first day to observe the proceedings. According to Sloman in *On the Road with Bob Dylan*, Hammond commented that it was strange to start the album on Rosh Hashanah: "Bob said, 'Well, why not today? It's the new year, isn't it?'"

The problem with starting the sessions on a holiday was the scarcity of available musicians. "I didn't see Bob until he came to the first session on September 16," Ramone wrote in his autobiography. "Earlier that day, Hammond called and asked if I could line up a few musicians. I didn't think the request was odd; I expected that Bob would just come in and lay down some voice and guitar tracks. But at the last minute, Bob decided that he wanted a few extra players. The New York studio scene was flush with work, and I was expecting to find that most of the A-list session players had already been booked."

It just so happened that an old acquaintance of Dylan's was cutting a jingle at A&R that day—Eric Weissberg, the multi-instrumentalist who a year earlier had soared to prominence with his hit recording of "Dueling Banjos." Weissberg first met Dylan in 1960 in Madison, Wisconsin, as Dylan was on his way from Minneapolis to New York City. Weissberg's ex-girlfriend was Carla Rotolo, Suze Rotolo's older sister. (Carla, an early champion of Dylan's folk career, was the "parasite sister" Dylan had excoriated in his "Ballad in Plain D.") A native of Brooklyn, Weissberg graduated from the High School of Music and Art in New York City, then went on to the University of Wisconsin–Madison and Juilliard School of Music. He became proficient on guitar, banjo, bass, fiddle, and mandolin and played with a number of prominent groups and musicians during the burgeoning New York City folk scene of the late 1950s. In 1959, he joined the Tarriers, a folk group that had two top-ten hits in the mid-'50s ("The Banana Boat Song" and "Cindy, Oh Cindy"), replacing founder Erik Darling, who left to join the Weavers and later formed the Rooftop Singers.

In 1963, Weissberg recorded an album called *New Dimensions in Banjo and Bluegrass* with future *Annie Hall* screenwriter Marshall Brickman and flat-picking virtuoso Clarence White, who would later join the Byrds. He toured and recorded with Judy Collins and made a traditional country–bluegrass album in 1969 with the Blue Velvet Band, which included banjoist Bill Keith, fiddle player Richard Greene, and former Blues Project bassist Andy Kulberg. Afterward, Weissberg found work primarily as a studio musician. In 1973, Weissberg was hired to play the banjo part opposite Steve Mandel's guitar on the song "Dueling Banjos," featured in the film *Deliverance*. The song was a slight reworking of "Feudin' Banjos," written in 1954 by Arthur Smith and performed by Smith and banjo player Don Reno. When the song became an unexpected smash—topping out at number 2 on the Billboard Hot 100 chart in March 1973—Warner Brothers sought to cash in by reissuing Weissberg's *New Dimensions in Banjo and Bluegrass* with the "Dueling Banjos" cut tacked on. That album went to number one and brought on a lawsuit from Arthur Smith, as Weissberg had been given credit for writing the hit song. The suit was eventually settled in Smith's favor.

Weissberg got a call from Dylan's office that Monday, asking him if he could return to A&R and bring a few instruments. Weissberg assumed Ramone was rounding up other studio musicians for the session. When he got there, no one else was around. "I finally reached Ramone on the phone and asked him who he got," he told Sloman for *On the Road with Bob Dylan*. "He said he tried everyone but it was too short notice and it looked like no one was coming. So I said, 'I got a band,' and just then Bobby walked into the studio and Phil asked Bob and he said, 'Sure, bring the whole band over.'" To capitalize on the unexpected success of "Dueling Banjos," Weissberg had assembled a touring band he named Deliverance, with whom he recorded the album *Rural Free Delivery*, released on Warner Brothers in 1973. Like Weissberg, the members of Deliverance were all experienced studio musicians who had played in a variety of groups.

Guitarist Charlie Brown III, born in Columbus, Georgia, had been a session guitarist with Atlantic Records in the 1960s and in 1970 released two solo albums, *Portrait of a Glad Man* and *Up from Georgia*, both on Polydor. Drummer Richard Crooks was a Californian who earned a BA in music from San Jose State and played in songwriter/producer Thomas Jefferson Kaye's band White Cloud. Their sole album, released in 1972, also featured contributions from Weissberg and Brown. Bassist Tony Brown had first appeared on the 1972 album *Music Among Friends* by a collective known as Mud Acres, featuring Maria Muldaur, Eric Kaz, and brothers Artie and Happy Traum (who had recorded several songs that appeared on *Bob Dylan's Greatest Hits, Volume 2*). Keyboardist Thomas McFaul studied music theory, piano, and trombone at the University of Illinois, then moved to Buffalo with a band called Time. They recorded one progressive/psychedelic album in Toronto called *Before There Was*, with McFaul on keyboards and vocals. He began doing session work in New York City in 1969, including playing keyboard on Charlie Brown III's *Portrait* album. In addition, guitarist Barry Kornfeld was invited to join the session. Kornfeld was an early New York folkie pal who in 1961 drove Dylan to the hospital to visit his idol, Woody Guthrie, who was dying from Huntington's disease. Kornfeld brought a metal-body National mandolin to the session but did not play on any of the takes.

Glenn Berger, Ramone's assistant engineer, recalled that first session in his autobiography, *Never Say No to a Rock Star*: "I set up for drums, bass, guitars, and keyboard. I placed Dylan's mics in the middle of the room. In the midst of the hubbub, Dylan skulked in. He grunted hello and retreated to the farthest corner of the control room, keeping his head down, ignoring us all. No one dared enter his private circle."

Before the other musicians arrived, Dylan recorded eleven solo takes of five of his new songs: "If You See Her, Say Hello," "You're a Big Girl Now," "Simple Twist of Fate," "Up to Me," and "Lily, Rosemary and the Jack of Hearts." All were strummed in open D turning on acoustic guitar with harmonica embellishments. According to biographer Clinton Heylin, Ellen Bernstein was sitting in the control room, and he seemed to be singing these songs directly to her.

Ramone recalled that the songs just poured out of Dylan as though he were doing a medley:

> Bob would start with one song, go into a second song without warning, switch to a third midstream, and then jump back to the first. Bob hardly ever played anything the same way twice, which was disconcerting if you weren't accustomed to it. On the first go-round he'd play an eight-bar phrase; the second time, that phrase would be shortened to six. The sessions were unscripted and unpretentious. I saw them as a spiritual release—a letting out

of the man's insides. When he stepped up to the mike and began singing, I saw a sensational album start to unfold.

Then Weissberg and Deliverance entered the studio. Glenn Berger wrote about the anticipatory mood in the room: "The studio cats, who spent their days and nights working with the best in the biz on groundbreaking shit and who usually embodied the essence of cool, were palpably pumped. It wasn't every day that you got to work with Dylan. You could feel the buzz in the room."

The buzz quickly dissipated, however, when Dylan began playing his new songs. Weissberg told Heylin that Dylan called the band to the center of the room, where he began playing and singing. "We scrambled for paper and pencils to try and scribble down the changes and the road map, etc.," Weissberg said. "I don't know which song it was, but it had a lot of verses, and we each got our own chart scratched out. Then I think we ran it down once, maybe twice, and Bob asked Phil if he was ready to record. . . . We did our first take. Bob asked for a playback. . . . During the playback, Bob called us to gather around him again and started to run down the next song."

As Charlie Brown III told Heylin for his book: "They had a live set-up for Bob, with a guitar microphone and a vocal microphone there in the room, and all the other guitar players and Tom McFaul, the organist, we were all right there behind him in the room. [But] they took Richard Crooks and put him in a drum booth. Now, in order to hear Richard, you've got to wear your headphones and Bob didn't want to wear headphones. So . . . you have to put Bob's guitar way up in the phones and simply follow him, which was not that easy, because he tends to shift tempos with his lyrics."

Any competent session musician can watch a guitarist's chording hand and figure out the key and the chords being used, but not only was the studio arranged so that several of the band members couldn't see Dylan's hands, but the chords he was playing were in open D tuning. At one point, McFaul tried to figure out the key they were playing in by going to the piano and sounding it out, but Dylan told him that he wanted organ, not piano, on the song in question. When McFaul told

Dylan he was just searching for the right key, Dylan repeated that he didn't want piano.

Weissberg described the situation to Sloman in *On the Road*: "It was weird. You couldn't really watch his fingers 'cause he was playing in a tuning arrangement I had never seen before. If it was anybody else, I would have walked out. He put us at a real disadvantage. If it hadn't been that we liked the songs and it was Bob, it would have been a drag. His talent overcomes a lot of stuff."

Dylan's preferred method of recording had always been to emphasize spontaneity over meticulous repetition. He valued the spirit of the moment over technical perfection, so it didn't bother him much if his backing musicians didn't know his material by heart. They were pros—they'd figure it out. But experienced studio musicians much prefer to be well rehearsed before the tape starts to roll and their performance is permanently captured. "Since mistakes had been made by each of us, we pleaded for another take, appealing to Bob in a nice 'We're on this record too, give us another chance to do it right' manner," Weissberg told Andy Gill, coauthor of his book on Dylan, *A Simple Twist of Fate*.

"It's not that he's wrong; it's just that it's a whole other way of thinking from what we were used to," Charlie Brown III told Gill. "He would run something down once, and maybe halfway again, and that was it: Take it! Because he wanted the immediacy of the moment—he didn't care whether there were mistakes in there or not; that's just the way it happened. We, on the other hand, were used to getting it right." Ramone was well aware of the session pros' mindset, and yet he also knew that Dylan didn't want to be interrupted or do multiple takes—and after all, Dylan was the client.

"I didn't get the message until about three-quarters of the way through the first day, and then I thought, 'Oh, I know what he's doing. He just wants to hear whatever comes out,'" said Charlie Brown III in Heylin's book. "We would go in [to the console room] . . . asking [Ramone], 'Can you get Bob to do this?' Whatever it was . . . Ramone never opened his mouth, never [even] responded. It drove me crazy."

In his autobiography Ramone professed amusement that he was later criticized for not being more sympathetic to the perplexed musicians: "My view from the booth, as someone who understood the artist in front of me, was that I needed to stay out of the way as the music came down. When Dylan walked into the room with guitar in hand, I knew that it wasn't about balancing the guitar against the vocal, getting a better sound on the guitar, or moving the bass player around. I instinctively did what I knew was right."

The six-CD collection *More Blood, More Tracks* that was released by Columbia/Legacy in 2018 included every existing take from the *Blood on the Tracks* sessions. The nine consecutive takes of "You're Gonna Make Me Lonesome When You Go" that were recorded near the end of the first session are clear evidence of Dylan's growing lack of confidence in Deliverance. As one take follows another, musicians appear and disappear, except for Dylan and bassist Tony Brown. Then Dylan and Brown take a first crack at "Tangled Up in Blue" and the session comes to an end.

Glenn Berger's autobiography aptly captured the developing mood of the evening:

> The excitement in the studio began to fizzle, like air leaving a balloon, replaced with fear and tension. No one would tell him he couldn't do this. After all, he was Dylan. But this was wrong. You're at least supposed to tell the musicians what song you are doing, let them learn the chords, and come up with an arrangement. You've got to give them a chance. One by one, the musicians were told to stop playing. Like swatted bugs, they writhed on the ground, waiting to die.... You could see it in the musicians' eyes, as they sat silently behind their instruments, forced not to play by the mercurial whim of the guy painting his masterpiece with finger-paints. The feeling went from tense to grim. We stole looks at each other, not understanding what was going on, not knowing what to do, hardly believing it. It slowly began to dawn on the musicians that the dream of playing on a Dylan record was not going to happen.

Still, both Ramone and Berger believed at the time that they had most of the album completed during that first day's marathon session.

In addition to the five songs Dylan had recorded before Deliverance joined him, they laid down acceptable versions of "Call Letter Blues," "Meet Me in the Morning," "Idiot Wind," "You're Gonna Make Me Lonesome When You Go," and "Tangled Up in Blue."

Nevertheless, the first night's session with Deliverance has to be judged a failure—or at least, given the final takes used for *Blood on the Tracks*, not what Dylan wanted. Only one of the twenty takes recorded that night made it onto the final version of the album: the first take of "Meet Me in the Morning," and that version was later embellished with an overdubbed pedal steel part played by Buddy Cage, the steel guitarist for New Riders of the Purple Sage, one of the Columbia bands Bernstein promoted.

Only bassist Tony Brown was asked to return for the second session on Tuesday, September 17. Dylan was going to stay with the open D acoustic arrangements of his songs but try for better performances. He did ask session pro Paul Griffin—who had worked with Dylan on *Bringing It All Back Home* and *Highway 61 Revisited* in 1965—to come in and play organ and piano on new takes of "You're a Big Girl Now," "Tangled Up in Blue," "Call Letter Blues," "You're Gonna Make Me Lonesome," and "Shelter from the Storm." In his autobiography Berger said that Griffin tried to "sunny up the date with his charm and smile. But he, too, didn't make the cut. His smile gone, he shrugged, and departed with his tail between his legs."

There was another musician in the building. Mick Jagger, who knew Dylan casually, was mixing live tapes of a 1973 Rolling Stones concert in Europe for a *King Biscuit Flower Hour* broadcast in an adjoining studio, and he found plenty of time to drop in on Dylan's session. On a take of "Meet Me in the Morning," Jagger suggested Dylan play a slide guitar part, but Dylan intentionally fumbled the lick as if to prove to Jagger that it had not been a good idea. There was talk of Jagger singing a backup part, but *Blood on the Tracks* was not going to be the kind of lighthearted album where rock stars do cameos. Both Berger and Cage were impressed by Jagger's pleasant personality but recalled that Dylan was not in a playful mood. "There was no rapport," Berger told Heylin.

"Jagger, who was super-charming, thought Dylan was 'weird.' He was unfriendly to Mick at best. The whole thing was short and it fizzled."

Of the recordings made that second night, only "Shelter from the Storm" and "You're Gonna Make Me Lonesome When You Go"—both featuring just Dylan on guitar and Tony Brown on bass—made the final cut for *Blood on the Tracks*.

Dylan was in the studio the following day to try four takes of "Buckets of Rain," but none of them made the final cut. The last day of recording in New York was Thursday, September 19, and the only musicians to record the twenty-nine takes during this marathon session were Dylan and Brown. They got a master take of "Buckets of Rain" and "Simple Twist of Fate," which completed the five New York recordings that would be released on the official version of *Blood on the Tracks*. With that, Dylan and Ellen Bernstein went with Jagger to Shel Silverstein's New York City apartment to drink until dawn.

In addition to the five tracks that ended up on the album, the sessions had yielded five other takes that made it to the album's test pressing: "Idiot Wind," "If You See Her, Say Hello," "Tangled Up in Blue," "Lily, Rosemary and the Jack of Hearts," and "You're a Big Girl Now." A couple of the selected takes—"Tangled Up in Blue" and "Shelter from the Storm" as well as the outtake "Up to Me"—were marred by the sound of the buttons on Dylan's jacket sleeve clacking against the surface of his guitar, but as far as Dylan was concerned, that was part of the ambience. He'd released other songs recently with the same blemish, including the "Main Title Theme" from his 1973 album *Pat Garrett & Billy the Kid*, and on the solo acoustic "Wedding Song" from 1974's *Planet Waves*. The sound of buttons on rosewood was not going to keep Dylan from meeting the album's scheduled pre-Christmas release date.

But despite enthusiastic critiques from his friends George Harrison and Robbie Robertson, and Columbia West Coast promo man Paul Rappaport, something about the test pressing didn't sit right with Dylan. Ramone and Berger were starting to sense Dylan's ambivalence. Berger wrote that Dylan called Ramone often. "I heard Phil say, 'Bob, it's amazing. Really, probably your best album ever. Don't worry. It's great.' Phil looked over at me with a perplexed look on his face. We shook our heads in disbelief. Dylan insecure? Huh? This went on, week after week, with Bob calling Phil for reassurance again and again as we approached the New Year deadline."

Ramone had prior experience with the lag time between a studio recording and its release. "Whenever an artist lets a recording lie around for any length of time, the temptation to redo—or add to what he or she has done—grows exponentially, and the impulse affected *Blood on the Tracks*," Ramone recalled. The Christmas holidays were approaching. Dylan was going to Minneapolis to spend time with his family, including his brother David Zimmerman, a musician, producer, and talent manager. Maybe David could ease his brother's nagging concerns about what could be the most important album of his career—or figure out a way to improve it.

2

"When Something's Not Right, It's Wrong"

DAVID ZIMMERMAN SHARED HIS BROTHER'S CONCERNS ABOUT *Blood on the Tracks* when he heard the acetate of the forthcoming album in December 1974. Although he has never publicly spoken about his reaction to hearing the New York sessions for the first time, he no doubt had similar suspicions that there wasn't a hit on the album. The critics might like the album—in fact, they might fawn over it as the comeback they'd been waiting for—but it was very unlikely to get much radio play or sell in significant numbers. Ten acoustic songs in open D tuning? That was no formula for a pop smash.

What was to be done? The album had been scheduled for a late December release, and Dylan's habit had always been to make his records quickly, release them as soon as possible, and move on to the next phase of his career, whatever that might be. Going back to New York for more recording didn't seem like a viable solution. But David Zimmerman had another idea.

Why not try recutting some of the songs in Minneapolis?

———

Minneapolis in December 1974 was a much different city from the one Bob Dylan left in December 1960. Back in 1960, Minneapolis had had no professional sports teams (the Lakers, a perennial NBA contender, had pulled up stakes and moved to Los Angeles that spring); no arenas or concert halls more modern than the Minneapolis Auditorium, opened

21

in 1927; no buildings taller than the thirty-two-story Foshay Tower, constructed in 1929; no interstate highways leading into the city from Bobby Zimmerman's northern birthplace or providing Bob Dylan's escape route to New York City. The only professional recording studio in Minneapolis in 1960 was Kay Bank, a converted vaudeville-era theater where local polka bands and jazz combos would cut singles at the rate of $495 for three hours of studio time and one thousand copies of their record.

The only recordings Dylan was making in 1960 were folk songs in the living rooms of his friends' apartments, but a few of his contemporaries, who stayed with the same rock 'n' roll music Dylan grew up playing, had found their way to Kay Bank studio. In the spring of 1959, Bobby Vee (with whom Dylan, as "Elston Gunn," had briefly performed in Fargo, North Dakota) brought his band to town and recorded "Suzie Baby" at Kay Bank. In the summer of 1960, a band called the Fendermen from Wisconsin re-recorded their novelty version of Jimmie Rodgers's "Muleskinner Blues" at Kay Bank, which went Top 5 on the national Billboard chart. At that time the former Bobby Zimmerman was an indifferent University of Minnesota student who was making plans to flee the Midwest, meet his folk-singing idol, Woody Guthrie, and begin his music career in New York. In the years since then, he had returned just once professionally, performing a half-acoustic, half-electric concert at the Minneapolis Auditorium on November 5, 1965.

By 1974, the Twin Cities area had become a modern, vibrant metro area hosting major league baseball, NFL football, and NHL hockey franchises; the Twins had brought the World Series to the state in 1965; the Vikings were on the verge of appearing in their third Super Bowl. There were new sports arenas in St. Paul and Bloomington, and a downtown Minneapolis concert hall. Interstate Highways 35 and 94 now intersected in the heart of Minneapolis. CBS's top-rated sitcom *The Mary Tyler Moore Show* was set in a fictional Minneapolis TV newsroom. Minnesota Public Radio had begun broadcasting a quirky variety show called *A Prairie Home Companion*.

The recording studio situation in Minneapolis had also changed dramatically. Kay Bank had continued to pump out hits with its three-

Herb Pilhofer at Sound 80 in 1971. Courtesy of Star Tribune Media Company LLC.

track echo setup, including Dave Dudley's country classic "Six Days on the Road" (1963); the Trashmen's unforgettable "Surfin' Bird," which topped out at number 4 in January 1964; the Gestures' Top 40 hit "Run, Run, Run" in late 1964; and the Castaways' catchy hit "Liar, Liar," which reached the Billboard Top 12 in the fall of 1965.

Tom Jung was the innovative engineer who recorded those hits and made Kay Bank the go-to studio in the Upper Midwest, even drawing the fledgling Winnipeg rock band Chad Allan & the Expressions (soon to become the Guess Who) to Minneapolis to record early sides. But by the mid-'60s, radio playlists had tightened, local and regional bands were having a hard time getting airplay, and recording studio techniques and equipment on both coasts were outstripping anything that could be done at Kay Bank. The solution to the studio problem eventually came in the form of a German immigrant and jazz pianist named Herb Pilhofer.

Pilhofer was born in Nuremberg, Bavaria, Germany, in 1931, and immigrated to the United States in 1954. His first wife was from the Twin Cities area, so Pilhofer settled in Minneapolis and began attending the University of Minnesota, where he eventually became a staff member. "In Germany I was sort of a big fish in a little pond, but when I came here, it was really quite an eye-opening, because I loved jazz, and it wasn't accepted here to the level—I thought in Europe, anyway—it should have been," Pilhofer said. "And so, it was a little bit frustrating to see highly talented people playing in a piano bar and nobody pays any attention to them."

Pilhofer formed a jazz trio, with guitarist Dale Olinger and bassist Stuart Anderson; they played at a club called Herb's in the 1950s and '60s. In 1959 he recorded and released the album *Herbert Pilhofer His Trio and Nonet* (subtitled *Music with the Modern Touch*) on the Audiophile label, featuring jazz standards by Duke Ellington, Thelonious Monk, and others. He also began writing music for other ensembles, and when the Guthrie Theater opened in Minneapolis in 1963, Pilhofer was named musical director. "For the seven or eight years I worked at the Guthrie, I had a chance to write a lot of music," Pilhofer said. "You know, I'd never seen a Shakespeare play in my life, and I ended up watching *Hamlet* twenty-five times. It was a good experience."

Pilhofer continued to compose and sporadically record, including orchestrating and writing the music for Richard Wilson's lyrics on a 1967 gospel-oriented soundtrack album called *What's the Meaning of This?* He also wrote sophisticated advertising jingles for many of the top companies in Minnesota. Since Kay Bank was the only viable recording studio in town, Pilhofer opened a small office in the building. When co-owner Vern Bank decided to sell his share of the business, Pilhofer stepped in to acquire one-third of the studio, with engineer John Michaelson buying the other two-thirds. The studio's name was changed to Universal Audio.

"I have always been interested in what a studio can do to making music," Pilhofer said. "It's sort of like a photographer in the old days, working in a darkroom, or today, working with Photoshop. You develop a basic idea or concept or piece of music and really push it into any number of directions, in terms of what the studio can offer." Pilhofer came to the conclusion that Universal Audio's facilities were not going to be adequate for the quality of recording he had in mind. "It was okay for doing some of the polka bands and some of the rock things that came in, but it wasn't anything that would measure up to what would be considered a studio on a national level," Pilhofer said.

He approached Tom Jung with the idea of building a brand-new studio from the ground up. He knew that Jung and several of the other engineers were frustrated that Universal Audio was not sufficiently upgrading its equipment. "It had never entered my mind [to start a new studio]," Jung told authors Dave Kenney and Thomas Saylor for their book *Minneapolis in the 70s*. "I said, 'Well, the first thing I would want is to bring some of [my] people.' Herb was 100 percent all for it. He said, 'That's your end of it. Whatever you want to do. I just want to build the best damn recording studio in the world, and do it in Minneapolis.'"

Pilhofer quit the Guthrie in 1969 to devote all his time to the recording business, and he and Jung recruited Universal Audio engineers Gary Erickson and Scott Rivard to join them. Erickson and Rivard built the new recording console from scratch, and they bought state-of-the art microphones, mixers, and tape machines. Initially, they operated a makeshift studio out of Pilhofer's living and dining rooms in Minneapolis. As Jung told Kenney and Saylor, the quality of sound they were getting at Pilhofer's house was far better than they had been able to achieve at Kay Bank, because the equipment was so much better. Yet a permanent site was definitely needed. "Quite innocently, we put on a tie, went to the bank, and presented a kind of pie-in-the-sky business plan, and basically got a loan," Pilhofer said. "The city gave us a piece of land [in the Seward South neighborhood of Minneapolis]. We each put $5,000 down and the rest was borrowed. We hired a very good acoustical engineer-architect, and with the help of some New York studio people, we ended up with a very good design for a studio that would serve the future."

The new 12,000-square-foot Sound 80 Studio officially opened in March 1971. The name Sound 80 was selected by advertising executive Brad Morrison, the man who had also come up with the name Cure 81 for Hormel's signature ham. "The name was picked without realizing how quickly the '80s would come up," Pilhofer said.

Advertising brought in the money—clients included 3M, General Mills, Wrigley, and Exxon—but Pilhofer always kept his hand in at composing and recording:

> I've done four or five jazz-oriented albums that I'm very proud of. They were never any big success of any kind, but I feel I've always had to do those kinds of things to satisfy my heart a little bit. The commercial stuff that paid you $2,000 for a ding-dong 30-second commercial was meaningless when you realized in the '60s I was commissioned from the Minnesota Orchestra to write a piece for orchestra and jazz quartet, which they performed and we did a couple of times. I got paid $200 for that, but I am so damn proud of that activity, and I wouldn't mention the commercial. It was a way of keeping your head oriented in the right direction. Sure, some things paid you well—but even the commercial stuff, I must say we got work for Mercedes, Audi, a lot of big-name advertisers, where we had the chance to do good quality stuff. It wasn't ding-dong jingles—I hated those. In some sense you had to do stuff that let you survive economically. We were very fortunate to do some things that you couldn't do anywhere else. I really think we lucked out in many respects.

Sound 80 also lucked out by hiring an engineer named Paul Martinson, who had been doing animated film sound for another local company. "The reason we hired him was that he had a lot of experience recording for film, and those are different needs and technologies," Pilhofer said. "Paul was so polite and quiet and unassuming, people liked working with him. He was known to be a technically very knowledgeable guy. In this business, when you end up sitting in a room with a guy for ten hours a day, you also look at their personality, whether you can stand him. Paul was a wonderful guy, very kind, very supportive, and he had a good ear for some things. This is a small town, so you know who works where. We were a small group; you try to find the best people in town to work with us. Paul was one of those."

Sound 80 was also beginning to attract pop musicians looking for the best recording facilities. Guitarist Leo Kottke was one of the first to benefit from Sound 80's expertise. Kottke was a native of Georgia but lived in a dozen different places before hitchhiking around the country with his guitar and finally settling in Minneapolis in 1966. He frequently performed at the Scholar, the same folk club where Dylan had played a few years earlier, and recorded his first album there in 1969. After recording his major label debut, *Mudlark*, for Capitol Records in Los Angeles, Kottke chose Sound 80 for his follow-up album, *Greenhouse*. The engineer on that session was Martinson, who was identified as "Shorty" Martinson on the album jacket, one of several nicknames the popular engineer accumulated during his career. He was also known as "Sprockets" and "Two," for the frequency with which he'd call for a second take. Martinson would work with Kottke on a total of seven of his albums, all recorded at Sound 80.

"Leo Kottke would only work with Paul," said Pilhofer, who played piano on several of Kottke's albums. "Paul had his followers, and that's very understandable. I worked with Paul in routine things I recorded. From a personal point of view, he was the greatest guy to work with. We were really fortunate at Sound 80 that we had people who worked with a passion for the music and for the content. It wasn't for the money. We never listened to an attorney or an accountant. We bought the best equipment we wanted to have, and somehow, we managed to make enough money to pay for it. It was a labor of love, and it came about at the right time. In the '90s you couldn't have done this."

"Paul Martinson was the consummate professional," said Jim Tordoff, a West Bank five-string banjo player who worked numerous sessions at Sound 80:

He absolutely mastered the recording equipment he was in charge of. He was very easy to work with. It was intimidating for me because I was basically just a kid banjo player. I'd go in and they'd sit me down in the room with the drums, bass and guitar. They'd say, "We'll just go through it a couple of times," and they'd give me a lead sheet to look at. It would be in the key of E-flat, because they were going to put horns on it later. E-flat is not a common banjo key. So, I had to quickly figure out how I was going to handle E-flat that day, right now. The fact is that the blood was not getting past my elbow to my hands, and I was nervous as a cat in a room full of rocking chairs about the whole thing. Then we'd go through it, and I'd sort of have a grasp of what was happening. Everybody would get up and say, "That sounds good," and after one take, they'd be done. I was sitting there with Paul, and we'd do it another three or four times. Then he'd say, "Okay, I have enough." He would snip, cut and paste back together again whatever they wanted for the banjo, because by that time I'd given them enough in-tune, in-key, on-rhythm stuff that they could put together whatever kind of stuff they wanted from my contribution.

Because of his work with Kottke, Martinson developed a reputation as an engineer who was particularly sensitive to acoustic music. That would soon pay historic dividends.

———————

Another Minneapolis figure who became quite familiar with the Sound 80 facilities was producer and talent manager David Zimmerman, who also happened to be Bob Dylan's younger brother. David Benjamin Zimmerman was born in Duluth in February 1945 and was four years younger than his only sibling. When the family moved to Hibbing in 1947, he shared a bedroom with Bobby, diligently took piano lessons, and eventually played in a Hibbing jazz trio. By the time David had graduated from Hibbing High School, his older brother had already changed his name and moved to New York City. When David started his own music career in Minneapolis, Bob Dylan was one of the most famous and idolized musicians in the world.

When he met with *Village Voice* reporter Toby Thompson in 1969, David Zimmerman was pursuing a degree in music education at the

David Zimmerman *(left)* and Kevin Odegard. Photograph by Barbara Odegard. Courtesy of Kevin Odegard.

University of Minnesota. The *Minneapolis Tribune* reported that "at the age of 22 David is 'eking out a fairly good career discovering, managing, teaching, and working with young performers.' He's very candid about the 'indispensable in,' that the fact he's brother to folk-rock hero Bob Dylan 'initially opened a lot of doors at Columbia' for him."

Zimmerman's initial break was working on Michael Lessac's 1968 Columbia album *Sleep Faster, We Need the Pillow.* Lessac was an actor and director who had been in residence at the Guthrie Theater in Minneapolis on a McKnight grant. He'd written a group of theatrical-sounding pop songs, and Zimmerman had assisted him and John Hammond (Bob Dylan's first producer) in assembling the musicians for the recording. One of those musicians was Minneapolis blues harp standout Tony Glover, an old Dylan pal from his University of Minnesota days.

Zimmerman's own career as a musician had come to an end, and by the early '70s he was a choir director, living in the Minneapolis suburb of New Hope with his wife and son. He continued to represent young, emerging artists. One of the acts in his Bernard Productions stable was a rock band named Skogie, a four-piece outfit fronted by Frederick "Rick" Moore that worked in the power-pop style of such groups as the Raspberries, Crabby Appleton, and Blue Ash. Zimmerman produced the band's lone single, "The Butler Did It" (b/w "I Won't Be Pushed Away") on the Mill City Records label in 1973. Moore would go on to marry a young actress named Demi Guynes in 1979; the marriage lasted only a few years, but Demi Moore kept his last name. Zimmerman also produced the single "July" (b/w "For Someone") on Mill City in 1973 for a vocal duo named Jesse. The backing musicians on that record were led by a local singer-songwriter whom Zimmerman managed, Kevin Odegard.

Though their levels of success were immeasurably different, Kevin Odegard and Bob Dylan had followed strikingly parallel paths: both were born and raised north of the Twin Cities; both were addicted to the exotic music from distant radio stations; both developed their performing chops at summer camp; both were in a succession of high school rock bands; both left their studies at the University of Minnesota to attempt musical careers in New York; and both released their first solo albums at the age of twenty-one. After that, their paths diverged significantly, but they were about to come together again.

Kevin Kerrick Odegard was born on September 29, 1950, in Princeton, Minnesota, a town of 4,500 on the Rum River, fifty miles north of Minneapolis. His great-grandparents, then spelling the family name Odegaard, emigrated from Norway in 1879. (*Odegaard* came from the name given to those who took over the Norwegian farms of owners who had died from the Black Plague.) Odegard's grandfather Odin ("named after the [Norse] god, though he was anything but," said Kevin in an interview) became a successful potato farmer in the 1940s, establishing warehouses all along the railroad tracks leading into and out of Princeton, where potatoes were extracted from the bogs, washed, and loaded on freights. Odegard refers to his grandfather, who served on Franklin D. Roosevelt's agricultural staff, as The Potato King, but it was his father who invented a variety of blight-resistant potato that could grow well in the excessively sandy soil found throughout Mille Lacs County. It became known as the Cherokee potato because it grew well in areas where the Cherokee Indians lived. "The government found it also grew in a much wider region and took over the patent," Odegard said. "My father called the sandy forest soil around Princeton the poorest you could find. We had what was actually called a sand farm south of Princeton."

The Princeton potato farms were partly tended by Italian prisoners of war during World War II. "They became acclimated, and were eventually welcomed in Princeton on Friday nights," Odegard said. "A friend of my dad's, who visited the bog on Friday and Saturday nights to cook pasta and serve chianti, recognized the maître d' of a restaurant in Italy."

Odin Odegard made a lot of money growing potatoes in Princeton, but it didn't last. "The prosperity of the family ended in the late '50s," Odegard said. By the 1960s the soil was worn out, and the family potato farm eventually became a Ford dealership run by Kevin's father, Robert, who then turned it over to Kevin's brother. Robert Odegard was twice elected to the state legislature and later became a fundraiser for the University of Minnesota, turning a foundation valued at $300,000 in 1971 into a fund valued at $2 billion when he retired thirty-eight years later.

Kevin Odegard was never interested in finances or button-down jobs. From an early age he was drawn to music. "I became interested in music when I was two or three years old," he said. "There are pictures of me looking at the giant family radio. I listened to the *Grand Ole Opry* on WSM, the *Louisiana Hayride* and all the southern stations. I was glued to that radio anytime I could pull in a station."

He came to understand that Princeton, situated as it was just one hundred miles or so south of the state's Iron Range, was a beneficiary of signals that were attracted by the iron to the north and bounced off the ionosphere. "I was listening to the same stations a kid in Hibbing was listening to," Odegard said. "I didn't find out till later that Bobby Zimmerman was doing the same thing. He must have driven through my hometown one hundred times on Highway 169 on his way to the Twin Cities."

Rock 'n' roll didn't make as much of an impression on him as the blues, country, and urban music that he heard on the radio. "I listened to Hank Williams more than Elvis Presley," he said. "The radio stuff I liked was the doo wop stuff by the kids from Brooklyn. That stuck out to me because it was great vocal styling."

Odegard also inherited some of his love of music from his family. His other grandfather, who served with Eddie Rickenbacker in World War I, was a violin player, and his mother was a concert pianist who never performed. "She got married first, but she would play in the house—Chopin,

Debussy," Odegard said. "I've never forgotten sitting at her feet and listening to her play. The house was filled with live, concert-quality music. That was a wonderful experience. My brother was a very talented trumpet player, into Mussorgsky, Haydn, Weber—he got very far into German composers. I would learn by sharing a room with my brother while he would play the classics."

And there was the pop music of the day. Perry Como was a favorite, partly because Odegard's grandparents lived across the bay from the TV and radio star in Stuart, Florida. Como's guitar player, Manny Godiva, would come over for weekly jam sessions, accompanying Odegard's grandfather while the adults drank martinis. "I still have all the sheet music in the house," Odegard said. "It's great fun to go through those standards."

Odegard's first instrument was a ukulele. He brought it to Camp Ajawah in Wyoming, Minnesota, every summer for seven years, entertaining his fellow campers in much the same way Bobby Zimmerman played for his friends at Herzl Camp in Webster, Wisconsin. Odegard discovered folk music in the early '60s, falling for the picking and harmonizing of groups like the Kingston Trio. The first record he bought was *Washington Square* by the Village Stompers. But he was not prepared for what happened to him—and millions of other music-loving kids—on the night that he watched the Beatles make their U.S. debut on *The Ed Sullivan Show*. "From February 8, 1964, I never had any other intention than to play music," he said. "The Beatles lit me on fire. When Abe Zimmerman made Bob promise to come back and go to school after a year in the music business, [Bob] never had any intention of going back. My dad didn't want me to go into the business any more than Abe Zimmerman did. But it was always going to be music for me."

The following summer at Camp Ajawah, another day became burned into Odegard's memory: July 26, 1965. "On that Sunday, I held a transistor radio up to my ear and heard 'Like a Rolling Stone' and my life changed forever," he said. "It was separate and apart from everything else we were hearing on the radio. I liked Eric Burdon and the Animals, I liked the Yardbirds. My mom would rescue me from camp to go see the Accents and the Underbeats and all the local bands, but when Dylan came on with that six-minute rant . . . ."

That was also the day a "pudgy little kid" wandered into his tent and introduced himself. Odegard was a fourteen-year-old counselor and Bobby Rivkin was a Cub Scout, but more important, he was the younger brother of David Rivkin, whom Odegard idolized as a guitar player in the Chancellors, one of the most successful bands in the Twin Cities. They'd had a number-one hit on the local charts with a cover version of the Righteous Brothers' "Little Latin Lupe Lu," and Odegard had seen them several times at the Spectacle Lake Ballroom. "I really was trying to use Bobby to get to his brother, because I was a huge fan," Odegard said. "I would sit at David's feet with the Chancellors at that ballroom, and he would make his Fender Stratocaster sound like the entire Byrds, with his double twin Fender amps. The ballroom was a roller rink during the day, and the floor would vibrate up and down because the Chancellors got the place going."

Bobby Rivkin would do all right for himself too. He later became the drummer in Odegard's KO Band and then went on to drum with Prince and the Revolution as Bobby Z. "I always remembered the day I heard 'Like a Rolling Stone' was the day I met Bobby Z," Odegard said. "We're still lifelong friends. We went through the whole Prince adventure."

Odegard's own adventures in rock music were about to start. He formed a series of bands, including the Auroras, the Nightbeats, the Mis ing Lynks (without the s, to be clever), and some that never had names. "People have sent me pictures of bands I didn't even know I was in," he said. "I was always in a band since the ninth grade. My first guitar had knobs that didn't do anything—they were just for show. Then I learned the Sears Airline was the better guitar; then I learned Fender was the way to go. I'd spend my paper route money on guitars and equipment. I knew how to play because of the ukulele."

Odegard enrolled at the University of Minnesota in 1968, nine years after Bob Zimmerman began his freshman year there. But the times they had a-changed. In 1959, the campus was a place for straitlaced kids to dabble in a bit of nonconformity by listening to folk singers at local coffeehouses. "I ended up living on the West Bank, but the coffeehouses that Dylan played weren't really going anymore," Odegard said. "There was nothing doing at the Scholar." By 1968, the West Bank had become a bastion of the psychedelic counterculture, with hippie clothing stores and underground record and head shops. Guitar in hand, Odegard embraced the bohemian atmosphere. "I jumped on the Bohunk bus with both feet," Odegard said. "I played the Whole Coffeehouse in the basement of Coffman Union. That was the biggest gig I played on campus. I was writing [songs], but most of all emulating, and trying to matriculate, but my heart wasn't in it. I tried."

He was the summer lodge manager at the Chi Psi fraternity house, which meant he had the minimal duties of filling the Coke machine and sweeping the floors. In his copious spare time, he built a recording studio in the basement of the lodge, where he re-created Neil Young's entire first solo album, multitracking all the parts himself on an Akai reel-to-reel recorder. Later that summer he stumbled into a job in North Dakota, thanks to a new friend of his, Stan Kipper, who was the drummer in a Minneapolis horn band called the Marauders. That band was managed by Mickey Johnson, who also recruited for an annual stage show at the Burning Hills Amphitheater in Medora, North Dakota, the one-time western ranch home of Teddy Roosevelt. "I was hanging around with Stan, and he [Johnson] picked me out of the chorus line and said, 'You look like a guy who could be a singing cowboy,'" Odegard said. "He sent me to Medora. I passed the audition and became one of the Burning Hills Singers."

For fifty-six nights in a row, Odegard sang cowboy songs and picked up some of the finer points of both performing and guitar playing. That's where he learned the value of a Martin D-28 acoustic ("the greatest guitar ever made") and the art of fingerpicking, taught to him by cast members Chuck Anderson and Steven Delapp, who would record and perform with Odegard in later years. In August, after the completion of one of their stage shows, Odegard and the other cast members watched Neil Armstrong walk on the moon. "I had just done the levitation act, where you swing a hoop over a body in midair," he said. "It's an S-curved brace, so you just thread the hoop through it. But backstage, Neil Armstrong was levitating to the moon. We went up into Teddy Roosevelt Park, built a bonfire, drank Everclear, and celebrated the man on the moon."

After returning to the University of Minnesota, he tried to generate some enthusiasm for his classes, but formal education just wasn't taking. Then in the spring of 1970, U.S. forces invaded Cambodia as part of the effort to subdue the Viet Cong, and college students went on strike nationwide. Odegard saw that as his cue to exit university life—and Minnesota. Just like Dylan did. "I would never admit to it, but I was emulating my hero," he said. "I'm glad I did that. He said some true things. Among them was, if you do what you love, that's productive for others and happiness for you. You can do whatever you want to do, you just have to get there and do it. Anybody can do and be what they want."

———————

Odegard wanted to be a singer-songwriter and make a solo album. Coincidentally, his friend Nancy Bundt was going to New York to see a friend who was deeply involved in Zen "intensives." "This was when we first met," said Bundt, who now lives in Norway and has had a successful career as a professional photographer. "He said, 'I want to come with you.' We drove to New York together and ended up living there for six months. You go with one pair of pants and one dress and stay for six months. But that's what you do when you're twenty, twenty-one."

They lived in the Village, familiar to Bundt because she had gone to New York University. Odegard got a job working at a music publishing company, and Bundt worked at an upscale store selling clothes until Odegard got her a job at the music publishing company doing covers for sheet music. Odegard was writing songs and recording them on a reel-to-reel tape recorder. Because their apartment was built over the subway, he had to record songs that lasted no more than two-and-a-half minutes, the time between subway trains.

Odegard played New Talent Night at the Gaslight, where Dylan recorded a live album in October 1962 (released for the first time in 2005), and performed in New Haven, Connecticut, with his friend from Medora, Steve Delapp, who was attending Yale Divinity School. Bundt had extensive contacts in the New York arts scene and introduced Odegard to Don Kasen, who ended up signing him to a recording contract with Wooff Records, a subsidiary of Peter Pan Records.

"We were heavily into yoga by the time we got to New York—swamis, breathing exercises, weekend retreats," Odegard said. "I met Liz Max, then wife of Peter Max [who would paint Odegard's portrait for the cover of his debut album]. The whole thing fell together because people wanted to do it. The vibes were cooperating. It all fell in my lap."

"That was through the same people that we met in New York at the Zen meditation place," Bundt said. "It was 1970—those were the times when people were connected to all that. If you were in the art or spiritual life, it wasn't that big, like now. Somebody knew somebody. Kevin had a lot of chutzpah; he just asked. And the guy said yeah."

To record demos for the album, Odegard was booked into Phil Ramone's A&R Studios—the same studio where Dylan recorded all his early albums. "I didn't know I was in a historic spot at that point," Odegard said. "I did demos there that turned out better than the record did. The demos were fun. They were an audition: 'How does Kevin work in the studio? How is his writing coming along?' Don Kasen wonders, 'Can I justify spending money on this album?'"

The demos strongly suggested the investment would pay off, so Odegard flew home to the Twin Cities in 1971 to record *Kevin Odegard* at Sound 80 Studios in Minneapolis. He returned with Nancy Bundt, who was now his girlfriend. "I was at MCAD [Minneapolis College of Art and Design] in art school at the time, and he was doing music," Bundt said. "We rented a farm for a while. We had a big barn and we bought three pianos for seventy-five bucks. All the musicians would come out and jam. We made videos—I made animations at art school about the band and we played it behind them while they played at the Walker. We were like twenty, twenty-one, doing pretty out-there stuff."

"You come home the prodigal son with an album, and you think you've just won the lottery," Odegard said. But having been away from the Twin Cities for a while, Odegard had to reestablish himself there and find someone to represent him. "I saw a story [about David Zimmerman] in the Sunday paper, and I said to my mom, 'I'm going to get David as my manager,'" Odegard said. He called a number of his contacts in the Twin Cities to put him in touch with Zimmerman, including Hennepin Theater Trust CEO Fred Krohn. "Fred once said to his sister, who took over his job, 'I'll give you a thousand dollars if you can say no to Kevin Odegard.' I could get on the phone and pitch. I will use every skill that God gave me to get to the objective."

Once the contact was made, Odegard still had to sell himself to Zimmerman. "Once I got David on the phone, I was nervous, I was shaking, but I evidently emoted enough. I had to drive up to his house in New Hope and sit with him on the lawn with his wife Gail and their son Seth. I sat on the lawn, picking blades of grass and talking about my vision, what I wanted to accomplish. It was not the same as what Bob was doing. I said, 'If you like these songs maybe we can do something together.' I never hit anybody over the head with something they didn't want, but I asked them to give me a chance. He and Gail accepted me in their family until we became pals. It was always about trust."

"David was a nice guy," Bundt said. "He was a really down-to-earth, nice person who really knew how things worked. He was very supportive of Kevin."

"David is supremely gifted as an arranger," Odegard said:

He's the opposite of Bob. He's the warmest guy in the world, very kind. He can't do enough for you. It makes sense now in retrospect. I went after him because of that. Once David and my mom met, it was gold. There was a relationship there. David's the brother of [a star], and my mom's a frustrated concert pianist. They had something in common: unrealized dreams and ambitions. I don't think he ever wanted to be in the spotlight, he just wanted to be in music, and enjoy what he did. Beatty [Zimmerman, Bob's and David's mother] taught her kids to be happy. Both of her kids were. And my mom helped. They became friends. They worked together to nurture my dreams. It was obvious to my mom where I was going. She had to give up being a concert pianist and wanted me to live the life she didn't get to live. My mother, David, and I spent a lot of casual time together, and we laid many plans as a team. I felt really protected and nurtured.

Kasen signed David Zimmerman to produce Odegard's solo album, and the team was assembled, all local musicians: Stan Kipper on drums, Steven Delapp on acoustic guitar, Andy Howe on electric guitar, Greg Anderson on keyboards, Richard Hiebler on bass, Max Swanson on flute, James Hauck on backing vocals, and Tony Glover on harmonica. "Tony was a wonderful big brother to me during that 1971 period of time," Odegard said. "That was Zimmerman's idea."

Sound 80 was selected as the site of the sessions because it was the best studio in the Twin Cities—and one of the best in the country. "An album can cost anywhere from $2,000 to $12,000 to produce," Zimmerman told the *Minneapolis Tribune* at the time. "Doing it here saved us money, in rehearsal and studio time, and was easier on everybody. We came in at $10,000."

But Odegard said the great feel of the New York City demos simply didn't transfer to the full-band sessions in Minneapolis. "The part with David was great; the part with the technical aspect wasn't so wonderful," Odegard recalled. "Most of it wasn't that much fun to make. I was back in hostage at Sound 80, working with an engineer I didn't enjoy [studio cofounder Tom Jung]. I liked the facility. It was a very focused place, but we were working with a guy we're stuck with. David was the one who always brought me back to earth. If you worry in the studio, it comes out in the recording. He would talk me through various issues and crises that I self-manufactured. There was a lot of excitement, because it was an opportunity that had great promise to it. The fact that it didn't work out took me to a new place."

Poor distribution and promotion often doom debut albums, but Odegard said that wasn't the case with his record. Kasen did everything he promised, providing wide distribution and decent airplay. *Billboard* magazine gave the album four stars, the album was described as promising and well produced by local reviewers, and it was distributed by Heilicher Brothers, owners of the Musicland chain of record stores. Chapman Distributing was promoting the album on the West Coast, and it received airplay in Boston, Memphis, Los Angeles, and San Francisco. Locally, album rock giant KQRS loved it. "KQ went bananas," Odegard said. "They played a lot of it, enough to get me some gigs. The long

Kevin Odegard *(center)* in the KO Band. Courtesy of Nancy Bundt.

one ['When I Get Home'] is really me just aping Neil Young. A reviewer said it sounds like a Jefferson Airplane jam. That's the one, oddly, that got all the airplay. I'd be on KQ for ten minutes."

WCCO-TV also used one of the songs on the album, a flute instrumental called "Krak's Song," as the theme music for one of their daytime shows. Odegard formed a duo with new friend and fellow guitar player Billy Hallquist, also part of Zimmerman's Bernard Productions stable. Hallquist cut a solo album called *Persephone* at Sound 80 in 1973. When Odegard put together his KO Band, he included Hallquist, old friend Bobby Rivkin on drums, future Glen Campbell music coordinator Jeff Dayton on guitar, and Gary Lopac on bass. Bundt was the band's number-one fan, photographer, and publicist. As she recalled:

> I used to shoot the bands back then. I'd shoot a lot of them, then make their posters. I'd go to the printer and make the things you'd staple to trees all over the place. I got fifty dollars for designing a poster and taking a picture. That seemed like a good deal. [Odegard] used to have me go to the gigs and bring my camera and flash. We didn't have a lot of money for film, so he'd just have me shoot a lot of flash so it looked like I was documenting, so it looked like something was going on, even though I wasn't shooting anything.

I thought that was really clever. I would shoot maybe a roll, then the rest of the night, just flash.

Odegard was making lots of friends in the music business, including another veteran of the Minnesota folk club scene, Seattle-based singer-songwriter Danny O'Keefe, whom Odegard would bring to parties whenever he was in town. But none of that translated into the kind of sales or performing opportunities that a solo performer needs to keep a career going. "One of the great things about Kevin was he expected the stars," Bundt said. "He did his best, he really worked hard at everything, and he expected it to succeed. And it often did, but at what level? You're in Minneapolis, you're twenty years old, what's going to happen? Unless someone brings you out to LA or whatever."

"I was running out of money," Odegard admitted. "I did a show at One Groveland, and my mother paid the musicians." Odegard was not too proud to face the truth of the situation: he needed another job until the music career picked up again. "I know a lot of people who are electronic engineers, who have degrees, and won't do it [take jobs outside their field] because of their definition of themselves," Odegard said. "They end up taking unemployment. I would take the job first. It was all I could do. I had no real college education, and I was not interested in the financial markets like my father. I was more suited at that point for adventure."

Some of the people he was hanging around with drove cabs, so like Harry Chapin's frustrated pilot in the 1972 hit "Taxi," he took a job as a cabbie. But he remained active. The jobs were sporadic, but Odegard kept his hand in. "The KO Band kept trying to break up, but we never really did," Odegard said.

"He dropped out of the university to go to New York with me, and I didn't think that was such a good move, because I knew he was really smart," Bundt said. "I thought it would be better to go back to school and let his parents give him money. But he didn't ask. He had that work ethic. That part I respected. I was at NYU for three and a half years and dropped out. I was in school at MCAD, trying to get my degree, and he was driving cab and playing music at night. He was doing both. I have a lot of respect for that. What kind of a job can you get at twenty-one with no college, with just your brains?"

By necessity, music had taken a back seat to Odegard's nonmusical obligations. At a Super Bowl party in January 1974, Odegard met Joe Stanger, a switchman with the Chicago–Northwestern Railroad who said the company was looking for good men to go out on the road. "That seemed much better than driving a Red and White Cab," Odegard said. "I applied, I got the job, and I lasted four years. It was one of the greatest jobs. Railroad is an inside job, handed down within a family, or else you have to know someone. If there's any other thing I should have done, it was stay on the railroad for thirty years. I enjoyed the people, it was good work, you stay active, and it's a good musical job: clickety clack, rolling down the track, swaying past the cornfields on a diesel. It's a great gig for someone who's always got music going."

The musical dream, however, was still alive. At one point, pal Owen Husney, a former bandmate with David Rivkin and Prince's future manager, went to a meeting with Odegard and the railroad trainmasters. "Kevin has a promising career in music," Husney told Odegard's bosses. "We'd like you to give him a leave of absence to pursue his dream."

"They gave me six months off," Odegard said. "I went on a college tour with the KO Band, then they welcomed me back. They kind of knew I was going to come back. I don't like to burn bridges. Keeping my band together while working on the railroad was not easy—they all had to be in other bands, other projects. The thing I always said to Stan Kipper is: I never had the courage to be a working musician because it's too damn hard to make a living. It's as much about practicality as courage. You can't make it on nothing. I never questioned that. I had to pay the rent, pay my bills."

Odegard was watching an episode of *Kojak* on the night after Christmas 1974—another very cold night in Minneapolis—when his phone rang. And rang. And rang. "I'm not picking it up," he said to Stanger, his roommate. "It's the railroad, and I don't want to go tonight."

Stanger understood. Working for the Chicago–Northwestern Railroad was a great job (paid well, steady work, good benefits) but sometimes the crew caller wanted an employee to drop whatever they were doing, regardless of the time of day or the foulness of the weather, and report for work on a freight headed to East Overshoe, Iowa. Odegard wanted to keep watching Telly Savalas suck on his lollipop and bust some crooks.

The phone finally stopped ringing, but then it started again. It rang, and it rang, and it rang. Then it stopped. Then it started ringing again. After a half-hour, Odegard couldn't take it anymore.

"Hello?"

"Kevin, it's David."

Well, that was a different story. "What's up?"

"I'm looking for a specific guitar—a small-body Martin, the 00-21 model. Preferably with gut strings. Do you know anyone who's got one?"

"What's it for?"

"I can't tell you."

Odegard's intuition immediately kicked in. There wasn't much that was off-limits between him and Zimmerman. If his manager was looking for a specific instrument but wasn't at liberty to explain why, it could only mean one thing: Bob Dylan was in town, and he wanted to make some music.

3

"Music in the Cafés at Night"

IT WAS NO SURPRISE TO KEVIN ODEGARD THAT BOB DYLAN WAS in the Twin Cities. He owned a farm in Hanover, thirty miles northwest of Minneapolis, and often spent time there during the holidays. It was a place for him to de-stress and relax with his extended family. Dylan had left the state years ago but always, privately, came back. His visits were never publicized, and he saw and talked to only the most trusted of old friends. No impromptu gigs, no club hopping, no star turns at ballgames or popular restaurants. When Bob was in town, no one needed to know. As far as his brother David was concerned, no one was allowed to know.

When Zimmerman called Odegard on that late December night, looking for a substitute for the stolen Martin, Odegard made one call: to the owner of the Podium Guitar Shop in Dinkytown, his friend Chris Weber.

Chris Weber was the only musician on the Minneapolis *Blood on the Tracks* sessions who was not originally from Minnesota. He was born in Pasadena, California, in 1947. When he was two, his family moved to Washington, D.C., where his father took a good job with his wife's family business. After a decade in Washington, the Webers moved to Florida. His father was a horn and piano player who had always wanted a family band, so he encouraged each sibling to play an instrument.

BLOOD IN THE TRACKS

"It just didn't click," said Vanessa Weber, who was married to Chris for forty-seven years. "Along comes Chris, he picks up a Martin ukulele at the age of three, and plays it easily." He began practicing and playing continuously after buying his older brother's guitar at the age of nine. "Fortunately, he had a good singing voice and was very much encouraged by his father," she said. When Weber was in the fifth grade, his parents came to the conclusion that the public schools in Florida were inadequate. His older brother was attending St. John's Preparatory School in Collegeville, Minnesota, where his father (a native of New Ulm) had gone to college. Though he had never visited the school, Weber was sent to St. John's Prep when he was in ninth grade. He had a brother who was a monk at St. John's Abbey, and a sister who was a nun at the convent, but he was not allowed to talk to them.

Though he never joined a rock band, Weber used his musical gifts to make friends. "When he was in high school, he was very popular, performing for the upper classes and the college," Vanessa said. "He firmly established himself as a solo entertainer all the way through high school. He stayed there through college. People felt immediately comfortable with him. . . . He was curious—always a people person." In August 1967, Weber won a talent contest at the Minnesota State Fair. First prize was a two-song recording session, at which Weber cut both songs with a violinist and a bass player. "They were good—kind of dumb, but musically very good," Vanessa said. "They were kind of protest songs."

Weber spent his first year of college at St. John's University in central Minnesota, then transferred to the University of Minnesota in the fall of 1967, where he met a fellow sophomore named Vanessa in a theater class. "Vanessa is my legal name now, but it didn't used to be," she said. "The teacher in that class called me Vanessa. When I told her that wasn't my name, she said, 'You look like a Vanessa. I'm going to call you Vanessa.' That's that. It was years before Chris knew it wasn't my name." They became good friends and started hanging around with the theater and music people. "He was dating someone else, and so was I," Vanessa recalled. "Close to the end of the class, we started dating. My sister had just died and he was a really good listener. We got to be really good friends before anything happened. He played music, and I fell in love with his voice. We started living together in 1969."

As Kevin Odegard was simultaneously experiencing, the University of Minnesota campus had become a counterculture haven, and Vanessa described herself and Chris as hippies. "He had long hair and was performing at the Whole Coffeehouse, and he had a regular gig at Fireside Pizza in Richfield," Vanessa recalled. "I was a real activist. I was out marching while he had started working at the Podium. He was enmeshed in that. I was in rehearsals, school, or work all day. We ended up living together because that was the only time we saw each other from eleven o'clock on."

Weber nearly left the Podium and Minnesota in the early 1970s. When he sang at the pizza joint, he would hear a beautiful harmony voice joining in on his vocals. It belonged to Polly Cutter, one of the servers at Fireside. Soon they became a duet. "It was a beautiful sound," Vanessa said. "Chris had been writing a lot of music—he didn't read or write music, but he could hear anything and play it right away. He wrote a lot of tunes. A guy named Joel Moss put words to some of them. It was working. Joel wanted to take him to California."

Weber and Cutter went into Sound 80 and recorded a dozen of his songs, which Moss put on a master reel to use as demos in California. "If they'd gone, they probably would have been very successful," Vanessa said. "They got as far as a contract, but Chris was concerned. He knew it would be impactful. I was going to go with him, but the traveling...all the bands were drunk, stoned, or high on something. The normal thing was to just lose your mind. He realized he would probably go that way. He decided between having us or the California Dream he'd rather have us. Also, he didn't feel real comfortable with the guy who wrote up the contract."

Polly Cutter did end up going to California and cut one single, "Ooh, I'm Satisfied," produced by hit songwriter Jeff Barry in 1975. She's also the voice on the theme song for the television sitcom *One Day at a Time*. She was a session backup singer when she quit the business in 1979. According to Vanessa Weber, she fell victim to the pitfalls of the business that Chris had feared: "Polly came back home because [the music life-style] was killing her."

After passing up a chance at fame, Chris and Vanessa bought forty acres of land for six thousand dollars in Wisconsin and built an A-frame house with no electricity. Chris suggested the couple throw a big party at their property. And while they were at it, he further suggested, they should get married. "I said yes," Vanessa said. "My father said he's not giving his daughter away in a cow pasture, so we had a formal wedding on July 7, 1973, then a hippie wedding the next day."

Shortly after they got married, they bought the Podium. It was not a great investment, a CPA told them later, but it was where Chris Weber's heart was. "We paid more than twice what it was worth," Vanessa said. "The blue sky, the good will—was extremely expensive."

The Podium, located in the heart of the University of Minnesota's commercial district known as Dinkytown, had started out as a sheet music and tobacco store, but Weber talked the owners into carry-ing guitars. "They were all acoustic and jazz guitars, beautiful instru-ments," Vanessa said. "It just took off. He was in his element, he was happy. His father said you don't need to buy something if you can fix it. He got woodworking tips from his dad and invented the setup. Kids would try to play, but it was impossible because the strings were too high, so they'd give up, thinking it was their fault." Weber would iron down the frets or fix the height of the saddle to make the instruments easier to play for novices. "He'd do a setup every time he sold a guitar. People would have it customized. Once we got known as having a very eclectic collection of guitars, and someone who could make it perfect for the individual, we had people coming in via word of mouth."

All the musicians in town knew Weber. Some, like Leo Kottke, would come to the shop and play for hours; others would just come to listen. Kevin Odegard was one of the many local players who fre-quented the shop. He recalled:

Chris was a scene-maker. He lorded over the folk scene from his post at the Podium, in the same way Izzy Young lorded over the

folk scene in Greenwich Village in the early '60s. He was our version of Izzy Young. You could hang around as long as you bought
a guitar pick now and then. There was some great talent in Dinkytown then. I lived on Fifteenth and University, just a short walk. I
spent many hours there when I should have been in class instead.
When you heard him play, the room went silent. He loved music,
loved the folk scene, from an early age. All I know is when I walked
into the Podium, he was in charge. He was warm, talented, and welcoming. He drew you to the place.

"Kevin was a rival on getting gigs," Vanessa said. "They worked in the
same circles, they were friends, but they kidded each other. Then Kevin
called Chris about a Martin guitar."

"Do you have this particular guitar?" Odegard asked Weber over the
phone. "I think it's called the Joan Baez model—it's a small-body Martin guitar, double-zero-twenty-one, something like that."

"We were specializing in acoustic guitars, and so we did a lot of
business in the used market, with Martins and so on," Weber said in a
2018 interview. "And so I got a call from Kevin saying that he was looking for a specific small-bodied Martin guitar."

The Martin 00-18 that was stolen from Dylan and the Martin 00-21
he had replaced it with were the same size, but the 00-21 has a slotted headstock. The model Weber had in his store was a 1930s-era Martin 00-42G (the G stands for gut strings, the preferred strings for that
model). It was very similar to the 00-21 with the slotted headstock.
Three days prior to Odegard's call, a young man had come into the Podium and told Weber his grandfather had passed away and left him the
guitar. "He said he had heard we were honorable and honest brokers of
musical instruments and asked if he could consign it," Weber said. He
agreed to broker a possible sale.

"Oh, you've seen it," Weber said to Odegard, assuming he'd been in
the shop in the past couple of days and noticed the guitar.

"What do you mean?" Odegard said.

"We have a 00-42, just exactly what you're looking for. But I don't own it. Why do you want it?"

"Well, I got a friend who wants to buy or borrow it."

"Who's your friend?"

"Well, my friend David called me up and he's looking for a guitar."

"David who?" Weber asked. "Is it David Rivkin?"

"No, it isn't David Rivkin."

"Is it David Zimmerman?"

"Yeah, it's David Zimmerman."

Forty-four years after that conversation, Weber could still recall going through the mental gymnastics of figuring out what Odegard was up to.

"I knew that Kevin knew the people in the Dylan camp and had some connection to them, and that David Zimmerman, Bob's brother, was his manager, or he knew him," Weber said. "I began to put it together in my mind, 'cause Kevin was being cagey as to who it was for. I thought, 'Oh god, this is a Dylan guitar, is what you're describing'—that classic Joan Baez model. Because they're smaller, they record well. I began to think, 'Holy cow, you know, maybe I'll get a chance to meet him.' But the underlying reason that I wasn't gonna part with it was because I was liable for a thousand dollars on consignment for this guitar. Now that may not sound like a lot of money for a vintage instrument today, but this is Christmas of 1974; that was like, you know, ten grand I was on the hook for. So I wasn't gonna leave this guitar." (In 2023, the asking price for a vintage Martin 00-42 could be as much as $100,000.)

"So he kind of had it figured out by then," Odegard said. "He said, 'Okay, here's my offer. I'll bring the guitar if I can come to the session.'"

Odegard called Zimmerman back with the good news. After going back and forth about whether Weber could deliver the guitar in person, Zimmerman finally agreed to let him come.

"Okay, well, here's the deal," Zimmerman said. "Bring it to Sound 80 tomorrow night at 5 p.m., and don't tell anybody."

"So this is for Bob, right?"

"I can't tell you that."

Bill Berg on drums and Billy Peterson on bass. Photograph by Steven Cohen.

Chris Weber. Photograph by Vanessa Weber.

But Odegard knew it was for Dylan, because he could practically hear Bob breathing over his brother's shoulder. Zimmerman finally admitted what was already obvious. He was looking to put a band together for a recording session. Odegard was stunned when Zimmerman asked him if he could recommend some musicians. Odegard began suggesting his friends.

"How about Stan Kipper on drums?" Odegard said.

"No, I've already got Bill Berg lined up."

"Doug Nelson is a great fretless bass player."

"No, I've got Billy Peterson on bass."

Berg and Peterson were the regular rhythm section on nearly every session—jingles, jazz, pop, rock—that took place at Sound 80. Zimmerman had worked with both of them and was convinced that they could handle anything Dylan threw at them. Odegard didn't know Berg, but everyone in town knew Billy Peterson, of the famous Peterson family. They were Minnesota music royalty.

Willard Oliver Peterson, always known as Billy, was born on January 22, 1951. He was the son of two accomplished pianists, Willie and Jeanne Arland Peterson, both of whom were staff musicians at WCCO Radio in Minneapolis. "My father was a great piano player," Peterson said. "His mentors were Bud Powell and Teddy Wilson, but he was also classically trained. He was groomed by our grandparents, Betsy and Ole Peterson—how Scandinavian is that? My father was president of his Minneapolis South high school class of 1939. He was supposed to give a commencement speech, but he had to go out to Glacier Park to conduct a big band when he was eighteen. I don't think he went to commencement. He was ensconced in music."

His mother, Jeanne, was also a singer, sometimes referred to as the First Lady of Jazz in the Twin Cities. Her parents were both pianists as well, and though she had no formal training, Billy Peterson calls her

one of the greatest natural musicians I've run across, and I've seen a lot of them. She was unbelievable. She had all these super gifts.

She could listen to anything and play it. She could listen to Oscar Peterson or Art Tatum and steal an arrangement off the radio. She showed me a lot of stuff—Dad didn't have the patience to teach me. She taught me something that changed my life. She played "Danny Boy" and said, "Here's the regular way to play it," then she reharmonized it and said, "Here's how I do it." I had to learn how to do that.

Jeanne Arland began playing piano by ear at the age of three and got her first job playing sheet music at Dayton's department store when she was fifteen. She was hired as a vocalist by WCCO in the late 1930s and remained with the station for twenty years. Her husband, Willie, was the leader of the WCCO house band. As Billy recalled:

Ever since I can remember, I was riding downtown to live broadcasts. Both my parents were on live radio, every day, up until 1960 [when WCCO dropped live musicians and switched to records]. I grew up in a sound stage with live musicians playing. I was exposed to music every morning, rehearsing new singers. I've got a recording of my father's duet with Oscar Peterson. WCCO was real progressive—radio was everything then. I grew up in that environment. There were people that would take care of me while they were on the air. 'Biddy' Bastien, Gene Krupa's upright bass player, would let me stand next to him while he was playing. He'd shush me, put his finger to his mouth, and say, "You gotta be quiet." I babysat myself, because I was so into the music.

Billy, the family's third of six children, was too small to play bass at first, so he began his musical education by playing piano:

I could play what I heard. I took keyboard lessons from an accordion player named Ernie Garvin, on staff with my parents. Then Larry Malmberg, father of Al [later a WCCO Radio late-night personality], a dear friend of my parents. He instructed me at ten, eleven, and twelve. I was getting started on the B3 organ and played drums, too. My dad in those years had live bands everywhere, so in the '60s he needed musicians. He hired me to fill in to be a drummer. I started playing drums with my dad because I had decent time. All through high school I could read music, play drums and bass in bands. Dad's bands were eclectic; we played schottisches, sambas, polkas, rhumbas—if you were going to be a working musician, you had to play every genre.

Like most male musicians of his generation, Peterson played in rock bands in the 1960s:

Jazz is my first love, but when I was a kid, I had a big amp and played electric bass all through that time. I loved Led Zeppelin and Hendrix. I had the first Hendrix album. I'd gone out to LA on vacation, heard Hendrix, and brought that record back. Nobody heard of him here. I was into rock, R&B—I could play any genre. I was in a high school band, but there weren't many guys that could play on that level. I'm not bragging, but I grew up so fast and played with so many musicians in my basement that I was blessed and advanced at a young age. I was self-obsessed with music. My basement was always open for anything—my parents let us rehearse there, so they would always know where we were. I used to rehearse with this great piano player named Mickey McClain. He had a big band, and my mom and dad would let me have the big band come in and rehearse in our basement in Richfield. That was 1967–68. The policy at my house was, "The door was always open."

Peterson became one of the regulars on his father's Rolodex of available musicians. "My dad needed me. He wasn't selfish; he farmed me out to his buddies." One of those buddies was a trumpet player named Jack Gillespie, a musical contractor who ran several different bands. Gillespie came to rely on Billy Peterson for a variety of assignments:

He put me out on the road with the Righteous Brothers in 1967, when I was sixteen. My dad was a contractor too. Sonny and Cher called my father for an appearance in Minneapolis. He hired the band. Cher didn't make it—she was having their baby. In those days, [recording artists] would go touring but wouldn't have a band. They'd pick up local musicians. Jack Gillespie calls my dad—I'm still in high school—and he says, "Billy can do all that rock stuff and read music." So I ended up getting the gig with the Righteous Brothers. Those guys were ten years older than I was. It was a real eye-opener for me to be on stage with guys at that level. I knew "You've Lost That Lovin' Feelin.'" I grew up knowing that. All the other stuff I didn't know. All of a sudden I'm caught up with all these screaming teenagers. I fell into that. I'd have to say being out, seeing what I saw, [the Righteous Brothers] were in their twenties with raging testosterone. I was pretty straitlaced. I had a great time, but I didn't partake. Most of the time I'd be traveling to another gig. My whole thing was taking care of business. I was a little kid from Richfield on these major tours. I just backed into it. Jack Gillespie would be in the horn section, so I was riding with Jack to these gigs. The Righteous Brothers' charts were all written out for the regional tours. The bands were always good. If I remember correctly, they brought a drummer. They'd carry a fragmented rhythm section, but they couldn't afford to bring everybody on the road to get the sound they had in the studio.

In the summer of 1967, at age sixteen, he landed a gig drumming for a big band that played weekends at a bottle club called the Downbeat on Lake Minnetonka. His cousins were in the band, as was saxophone player Bob Rockwell, who would later join him in a jazz-fusion group. "We had a smokin' big band all summer," Peterson said. "Through high school I was reading Buddy Rich kind of charts. That's where I cut my teeth reading music, on the more jazz-type stuff. I played there between sophomore and junior years, but after high school, I couldn't do it that summer because I was too busy with my dad's band. I knew I wasn't going to go to college."

Peterson was supposed to graduate with the Richfield High School class of 1969, but like his father he did not attend the commencement ceremony, but for a different reason: he missed so much school while

53

Billy Peterson. Photograph by Bill Berg.

touring with different bands that he didn't have enough credits. "I was into sports," Peterson said. "I played baseball, but I didn't take care of my education." He was simply too busy becoming a world-class musician. He wasn't worried about his future, however. He married a year after high school, worked constantly, and made more money than any of his classmates. "I was playing with my dad's bands all the time," he said. "A lot of different people would call me. Those guys knew what I was capable of doing. There were so many bands out—every bar had a band. If you didn't have a band, you couldn't keep a person in there. I was just a jobbing musician—bar mitzvahs, etc. When I was playing with my dad's band, I'd make $45 a gig. Every weekend I had almost $100 in my pocket, an astronomically large amount."

The money got even better when he committed to steady gigs with jazz groups. In 1971 he started playing six nights a week at a jazz club in downtown St. Paul called the Take Five Lounge. "A great jazz club—it was packed every night," Peterson said. "I had my twenty-first birthday in that bar. That lasted for a few years. Then I met these great musicians: Irv Williams on sax, and Billy Wallace, a great piano player who was Clifford Brown's piano player in Chicago. We had a gig in the revolving carousel restaurant at the St. Paul Hilton. They hired me, this little kid from Richfield, to play bass. I was the luckiest kid on the planet. These guys had the patience; they showed me everything. I had that gig with Irv until 1973. I was rolling in dough. I had two cars, I bought a house, we had a kid. I grew up really fast."

He also played with drummer Kenny Horst, future owner of the Artists' Quarter jazz club, at a Minneapolis club called Davy Jones' Locker. "All these gigs were crossing. I'd be running all over the place, playing with Kenny, playing with Irv." He found time to work in a bar on Hennepin Avenue in downtown Minneapolis called the Poodle Club. That's where he formed the nucleus of his own group, Natural Life, along with Bob Rockwell on sax, Steve Kimmel on percussion, Tommy O'Donnell on piano, Mike Elliot on guitar, and a drummer named Bill Berg. "I probably met Bill in the early '70s," Peterson said. "We started doing jam sessions together, just getting to know each other. Then Bill and I were hired by Herb Pilhofer to be the house rhythm section at Sound 80. We were super tight. That's what people have told us. We had a great synergy, having played many sessions together."

––––––––––

William Arthur Berg was born on December 29, 1945, in Hibbing, Minnesota. He'd never met Bobby Zimmerman, as Bill Berg was four years younger, but he'd seen him once onstage in Hibbing, playing with his rock 'n' roll band the Golden Chords. "It wasn't something I thought was great," Berg recalled. "I was much more listening to jazz at that time. It didn't go over well—not a big round of applause. It struck everybody as 'We don't get it.'"

Berg had developed his musical appreciation at an early age. It started with listening to his father's collection of jazz and pop 78s. His father, Roy, was an accountant for iron mining companies by day, but by night he was also an excellent jazz piano player and singer. He played with jazz quartets and quintets all over Minnesota's Iron Range—Ely,

Virginia, Buhl, Grand Rapids, "anywhere up in the north," according to Berg. "If they did get to Duluth, it was a bit of a stretch for them." Berg's brother discovered some posters of a big band their father had played in that toured the Dakotas and northern Minnesota in the '30s and '40s.

Like many jazz devotees, Roy Berg didn't care for the rock 'n' roll sounds that were taking over the radio in the 1950s. "He was strictly jazz, classic jazz, Duke Ellington, Frank Sinatra stuff, and all the pop of that '40s–'50s era," Berg said. "That's as far as he would go—although when I introduced him to Blood, Sweat & Tears and Chicago, he heard the more sophisticated chords and horn arrangements. That got him. He enjoyed Miles Davis, like a lot of the older guys liked the '50s bebop era. But the minute Miles went fusion, which all of us younger guys loved, he never got into the fusion genre."

Berg's mother was from Ely, Nevada, but her parents had initially tried living in Hibbing after coming to the United States from Croatia to find work at the world's largest iron ore mine. "They knew the iron ore thing was starting to happen," Berg said. "That's what brought my grandfather and his wife, but they came separately. They checked out Hibbing and were not totally enthralled. That took them out to Nevada to mine, but they didn't like that either, so they came back and settled in Hibbing."

Berg's father was originally from Crookston, two hundred miles west of Hibbing, but was working at the Hibbing Municipal Airport in 1943 when somebody set him up with his future wife. They married and bought a house that had been moved from North Hibbing when the Oliver Mining Company discovered that some of the deepest veins of iron ore were under the buildings of North Hibbing. "Our house had a down-and-dirty foundation," Berg recalled. "I think we always had some little problems with shifting or a basement that was rocky. We had anything but a flat floor."

Berg remembers his father's quintet playing live concerts at Hibbing's movie theater. "He'd bring me to rehearsals," Berg said. "It was small arrangements, two horn players, upright bass, piano, and guitar." Berg gravitated toward the drums. His father arranged for him to take lessons with a jazz drummer named Dick Collyard, but when it came time to buy a kit, Roy Berg proceeded cautiously. "A lot of people nowadays, the minute they hear a kid has interest in the drums, they'll go buy them a multi tom-tom and cymbal kit, and the kid will quit in a week," Berg said. "My dad bought me an old kit for sixty bucks—giant calfskin heads, somebody else's name on both sides of the bass drum. It was rickety, but it was mine. I played them probably four or five years. My dad said he knew I needed a better set, but it happened along with summer jobs, mowing lawns, planting flowers for a buck and a half an hour."

Berg eventually bought a good set of Ludwig drums. Like his father, he was more into jazz than rock, but he used to take the sixty-mile trip to Duluth to see the battle of the bands at the National Guard Armory. He knew which way the musical winds were blowing. "Here comes Buddy Holly and Elvis, and as a young kid I knew what the girls and guys liked," Berg said. "When I went to the youth center in Hibbing, I already figured I'd better learn this rock and roll stuff."

He played in the junior high school and high school bands, practiced at home with records, found others who liked to play, and put a band together. Then he was asked to join a rock 'n' roll band called the Classics from nearby Chisholm. Consisting of electric bass, rhythm and lead guitars, and drums, the band was hired to back up pop vocalist Bobby Vinton ("Roses Are Red," "Blue Velvet") on his tour of the upper Midwest in 1962. Berg was just sixteen years old when he hit the road. "He was a good musician," Berg said of Vinton. "He graduated from Duquesne University as an oboe major. He could also rock on really bluesy, up-tempo things, whatever it was. We kicked butt out there."

They were out most weekends, playing dance halls and ballrooms in Minneapolis, Des Moines, Albert Lea, and other regional stops. When he first joined a band, Berg had been happy to get ten or fifteen dollars for a three-hour gig, but on the road with Bobby Vinton he was making between fifty and seventy-five dollars a night. There was no tour bus; instead, they traveled in the bass player's station wagon, pulling a trailer. "Bobby would ride with us," Berg said. "For my first touch with a star, Bobby was really nice, really supportive. He appreciated how good we were—and we were a pretty good band for northern Minnesota."

When not backing Bobby Vinton, the Classics played teen dances and proms, starting as a quartet and later adding a female singer. They opened for the Trashmen a couple of times in Hibbing. Their repertoire consisted of songs by teen idols like Dion, Ricky Nelson, Elvis Presley, and Del Shannon. "We tried to do Chuck Berry or Little Richard, but we were a little too white to dig into the depth of rhythm," Berg said. "Even though I was pretty shy, it seemed like I was getting a little notoriety. I was not the great quarterback or the basketball player, but I was being noticed."

In 1964, when Berg was a senior in high school, he joined a Hibbing band called Little John and the Sherwood Men. They went to Kay Bank Studio in Minneapolis to record an original surfing song called "Movin' Out," sung by bassist "Little" John Hamilton and engineered by Tom Jung. "That was one of the funnest bands I've ever played in," Berg said.

Berg and Hamilton also played regularly in a jazz trio with one of their classmates who played a pretty fair piano, David Zimmerman. "Dave was more a classically based piano player, pushing into jazz-pop," Berg said. "We did 'Pink Panther' and pop hits that would lend themselves to sort of a jazz rendition. We played some little parties, a few little things." During a rehearsal in the Zimmerman's basement, David told his bandmates that he wanted them to hear something. He put on one of Bob Dylan's early albums and said, "This is my brother." It was difficult for Berg to make the connection between the would-be rock 'n' roller he'd heard wailing on the Hibbing High School stage some five or six years earlier, and the strident folk singer he was listening to in that basement. "All I ever heard was crooners like Frank Sinatra and Dean Martin, and rock guys like Elvis," Berg said. "Bob's voice was thoroughly unique. To me it was a stretch to get what he was doing. It didn't take me long to realize the depth of his lyrics and how earth-moving those were. Once I got past the quality of his voice, I started to appreciate what an artist he was."

The jazz trio didn't last long, because Berg had decided to leave Hibbing for art school in Chicago. "I had a real yearning to be a magazine illustrator," Berg said. "I chose to go to the Chicago Academy of Fine Arts for two years. I put a number of different animal drawings and still lifes in my portfolio, and it was good enough to get in. It was a starting point for me."

Art school kept him too busy to join a band or even play very often, but he did bring his drum set with him. He put blankets and towels on his drums so he could play them in his small apartment without bothering the neighbors. "It was frustrating," he recalled.

> I got a couple gigs. I took drum lessons at Roy Knapp Drum School where Buddy Rich, Gene Krupa, and the more famous drummers went to school. Roy Knapp was getting up in years, so I studied from another Chicago drummer there named Gene Ciszek. Because he was really a good all-around player—rock, jazz—I put things together from watching him play. If you put somebody in a room with somebody ahead of you in years and technique, you really learn. He had books that were really appropriate for my level of expertise. I went to see him play at a burlesque house on the near north side of Chicago. I felt way out of my comfort zone, but he was really controlling the band, and I thought, "Wow." He did everything right.

After two years in Chicago, Berg moved to St. Paul and started work as an illustrator in an art studio called Creative Art Service. He did a variety of jobs, including packaging, illustrating, design, and 3M product artwork. "When you're in an art studio, you do everything that comes in the door. We didn't have computers that printed out type. We had to paste up any kind of type that described the product or told the story—cut it with an Exacto knife and put it on boards. At that time, I knew that would be my day gig, but as I've done just about all my life, I did the music and the art at the same time."

Berg's beginnings as a professional illustrator coincided with the height of the war in Vietnam. When the first draft lottery was instituted, he drew a low number and knew he'd be selected. "It was either army infantry or audition for one of the Navy bands," Berg said. With Navy bands in every major port, including San Diego, San Francisco, Newport, and Jacksonville, Berg correctly assumed there would be a spot for him. He got into the Armed Forces School of Music in the Norfolk, Virginia area and was initially stationed in Memphis. Then he was assigned to the U.S. Naval base on the island of Guam, where he stayed for a year and a half. He put together a couple of jazz-fusion bands on Guam and enjoyed the spectacular snorkeling, but he also had some memorable service moments. "One of the big honors in my life was playing for the Apollo astronauts a couple of times when they would splash down in the ocean nearby," Berg said. "I played for Nixon on one of his visits to China when he was president. That was more than fifty years ago, and the island has changed a great deal, but we had a lot of fun. I met many fabulous musicians who, like myself, did not want to go into the army—players from the Buddy Rich and Woody Herman big bands," Berg said. "Being a small Navy band of sixteen to twenty pieces, we had to do everything from concert music to big band and jazz combo. I got a great education playing a lot of different kinds of music."

When Berg got out of the Navy in 1970, he returned to the Twin Cities, where he joined up with his old Hibbing buddy John Hamilton and put together a rock band called Juba, a name taken from an old Western movie: "We played all around Minneapolis. The most memorable gig was a bar across the street from a slaughterhouse/meatpacking plant in St. Paul. It was a real blue-collar crowd, and they didn't exactly love our deep cuts from Jethro Tull albums. Every time we took a break they applauded when we left the stage and turned the Twins game back on. And I'm thinking, 'Oh, man, is this a business I want to stay in?'"

By 1971 Berg had begun playing in a jazz-fusion group called Passageway with pianist Gary Brunotte and electric bass player Ted Nierowicz. They played the Holiday Inn circuit and jazz clubs in the Twin Cities area. "Minneapolis has always had a real good resident group of jazz musicians, and there were always clubs available," Berg said. "The clubs come and go. Any jazz musician anywhere in the country has to do research and see where they can play jazz instrumental music."

Playing fusion in Twin Cities jazz clubs was where his path crossed with Billy Peterson, who was pursuing a similar sound. "I knew he was part of the Peterson family," Berg said. "He was working in St. Paul when I went to see him. I sat in with the band, and we said, 'Let's start playing

Bill Berg. Courtesy of Bill Berg.

together.' He and I started to work together putting a fusion band to-gether, playing a couple of restaurants in Minneapolis."

In addition to getting steady work with their new band, Natural Life, Berg and Peterson began playing together on recording sessions. "He was one of the principal bass players at Sound 80," Berg said. "Billy was the instrumental guy getting me in there to work with Herb Pil-hofer and Tom Jung. We did so many sessions there. The first one was probably a local bank ad. Then we did Northwest Orient commercials and Mutual of Omaha. I absolutely loved it, not only the jingle work but the requirements of being a good reader and knowing a number of styles of music. That led to other work: gospel and country records and local folk artists. That's how I met the late Lonnie Knight, and the late, great Michael Johnson. Both of them played sessions too."

Berg found himself doing session work two or three times a week, and sometimes every day. "It certainly supplements your income," he said. "Even though some of the people you play with in the jazz idiom will put you down: 'Oh, you went to do a Dairy Queen commercial to-day?' There was a little bit of that from the jazz community, but it didn't bother me at all. I could go out and be a fusion musician and still do a Northwest Orient commercial. I definitely made more money doing jingles. In those days you'd be on a thirteen-week cycle: if they renewed the commercial, you'd get royalties from that. If a certain company wanted you to play on their jingle, they'd do the royalty thing or offer a buyout at a higher figure, which means you get paid the first time and not again."

In addition to his work with Peterson as the rhythm section at Sound 80, he was often hired to work at Cookhouse, the new name of the former Kay Bank Studio. "I would work with a really good performer and musician, Dale Menten, who hired me a whole bunch," Berg said. Menten, lead singer and songwriter for the Gestures, who had a Top 40 hit with "Run, Run, Run" in 1964, had bought the old Kay Bank Studio and was now heavily involved with commercial and industrial music production. Cookhouse was a busy and creative shop, but Berg's technical side appreciated the extra care that had gone into creating and building the Sound 80 studios. "It was a state-of-the-art complex," he said. "They had some sort of a floor that actually was suspended to some degree so the vibrations of the room would not be a negative, so the low-end bass would not affect the overall outcome of the music. Just based on what I heard from Tom and Herb and some of the engineers, it was all cutting edge: 'What can we do to make the sound better?'"

Billy Peterson describes the core Sound 80 musicians: he, Berg, bassist Jimmy Johnson (now the bassist in James Taylor's band), and keyboardists Billy Barber and Herb Pilhofer as the Wrecking Crew of the Twin Cities. "We had a great rapport," Peterson said. "We could do any genre of music, any style of music, and do it authentically. We were lucky to do that, and we were called to do that a lot."

Berg and Peterson backed pal Bob Rockwell and keyboardist Bobby Lyle on a jazz-fusion album called *Androids*, recorded at Sound 80 in 1974 (Berg also did the cover illustration). The first major label release Berg and Peterson worked on at Sound 80 was Leo Kottke's *Dreams and All That Stuff*, released on Capitol Records in 1974, with Paul Martinson engineering. "We started working with Leo Kottke in 1974," Peterson said. "That prepared me and Berg for working with Dylan. Leo's a great player, a real original. When Dylan came in, we knew what he needed to make his stuff pop."

Martinson's experience with Kottke also made him the ideal engineer for the Dylan sessions. "I'd worked with Paul often," Berg said. "The engineering job was split up between Tom Jung, Scott Rivard, and Mr. Martinson. I think he was one of the most relaxed and supportive engineers I've ever worked with. Given any situation, maybe a jingle we'd do, there might be a producer or the jingle writer who was uptight, unsatisfied with the rhythm section—maybe he thought it was too busy—any number of things, and Paul would come in and soothe the waters every time, make things workable, with a relaxed smile on his face all the time. He was so good. He was like a lot of guys who'd worked at smaller studios and had to do everything—assistant engineering, running for coffee."

Zimmerman chose Martinson to run the controls for the December 27 Dylan session. "David told me Bob was going to record some songs at Sound 80," Martinson told music journalist Andy Gill. "He didn't say how many—at least one or two. . . . I felt I had been chosen by David to do this because he and I had done a number of things before. So I knew he had confidence in me."

In Peterson and Berg, the rhythm section was set, though only Berg was told that it would be a Bob Dylan session. As it happened, Berg was preparing to leave the Twin Cities for Los Angeles shortly after Christmas. He had bowed out of Natural Life (replaced by respected jazz drummer Eric Gravatt), and his Volvo station wagon was packed with his personal belongings; attached was a trailer that contained his records and his drums. He might have already left town by that Friday, had it not been for the opportunity to play with Dylan. "My intent was to go to California after I felt I'd done everything musically I could do in the Twin Cities," Berg said. "After working at Cookhouse and Sound 80, playing in a number of bands, I felt I wanted to try the West Coast. I had my car pretty much packed to go west to California. It was my last few days living in Minneapolis. Then here we go: I got a call from Bob's management."

Zimmerman simply called Peterson on Thursday and asked him to be at Sound 80 Friday night, without telling him why. Peterson figured it was a jingle session, which would leave him plenty of time to get downtown for his regular weekend gig with Natural Life. "We'd get calls all the time from him, just spur-of-the-moment things," Peterson said. "We'd pick up the phone: 'Hey, can you be in the studio tomorrow? I got some . . .' You know, we're young, we got families, we're trying to make some money, right? So David was real good to us in those days."

With Dylan, Odegard, and possibly Weber, there would be plenty of guitars at the recording session. The one missing piece was keyboards. Dylan had tried Paul Griffin on the New York sessions but was not satisfied with the tracks he'd played on. Herb Pilhofer often filled in on keyboards when needed at Sound 80, but a more rock-oriented style was called for here. Odegard suggested they invite a friend he'd been working with recently, a former hard rock guitarist who'd become a fusion keyboard player in a local band called This Oneness: Gregg Inhofer.

Zimmerman agreed, and the band was set.

4

"Heading for Another Joint"

GREGG INHOFER HAS PLAYED WITH SO MANY BANDS AND MUSI-cians in the Twin Cities and elsewhere, going back to the late 1960s, that it would be hard to find a player he didn't know. He can't remember when he met Kevin Odegard. He assumes it was for some long-forgotten gig when Odegard needed a keyboard player. "It could have been through Stan Kipper, who was his drummer," Inhofer said. "I've known Stan since he was in the Marauders, with Doug Maynard as the lead singer."

Greggory John Benedict Inhofer was born at Swedish Hospital in Minneapolis in 1950, to a devout Catholic family. "I have a confirmation name," Inhofer said. "I wanted Fabian—because of [pop singer] Fabian. I found out that Fabian and Sebastian, who were probably gay, were both shot with arrows and became saints." Inhofer's two sisters, who are Benedictine nuns, said no. "You're going to be Benedict," they decreed.

Inhofer's father was originally from the heavily German area of New Ulm, Minnesota—like Chris Weber's father. After failing at farming, the Inhofer family moved to Minneapolis. "I believe I got my musical ability from my mother," Inhofer said. "I never heard her sing in my whole life. When she was a child, she took violin lessons and her brother took piano lessons. He took them because their parents told him to. The story was, she was pretty good, and getting better. But money got tight in the 1920s, and whose lessons go? The girl's. She never picked it up again, never played an instrument, but I think that's where it came from."

Inhofer remembers exactly when he got interested in music. He was eight years old, and his Uncle Orey ("who was the black sheep of my mother's family—my mother was always the one who took in the wayward brothers, and he was the one that had a drinking problem") shared a room with Gregg. "Me and Uncle Orey and his stinky feet," Inhofer recalled. "So he had given me a plastic trumpet. He gave my sister a little plastic chord organ. I pulled that puppy out of the box— never touched an instrument before, and I went [mouths 'Taps.'] I was amazed, everybody was looking at me, and I went, 'Wow.' I was hooked. All of a sudden the old acoustic guitar in my other uncle's attic took on a new meaning."

The next time Inhofer went to see that uncle (who was also his god-father) he got the guitar from him. One of the priests from their church taught him some cowboy chords. "I played that for a little bit," Inhofer said. "But I just started to do stuff. I was playing pots and pans along with an old Victrola that a friend of mother's had given me. There were two records that I liked. One of them was a foxtrot record that I played the pots and pans with: 'Root-doot-doot-do . . .' And the other one was a [comedy] record called 'The Old Country Gentleman in New York.'"

He started kindergarten at age four, due to a clerical error, and it had long-lasting repercussions. "My birthday's in November and I should have been refused," Inhofer said. "You're supposed to be five by the end of September or something, but I slipped through, and it was detrimental my whole life. I was always the youngest. I was the last one to do things, the last one to mature, the last one to drive—you know, everything. So it sucked."

Inhofer might also have been one of the last kids of his generation to get hooked on rock 'n' roll. Instead of listening to Top 40 radio in the late 1950s, he was finding other forms of stimulation for the creative— and humorous—impulses that have fueled his career for half a century. "I was watching *Winky Dink* on TV," he said. "For two corn flakes box tops and fifty cents you could get a Winky Dink kit, which consisted of a heavy-duty plastic screen with the outline of a TV screen on it, and a Winky Dink wiper cloth and a Winky Dink crayon. 'Winky Dink! Oh no, the bridge is out! How is Winky Dink going to get across the river?' And you'd draw a bridge. And I always used to think, how many kids were drawing devils and pitchforks and flames, going, 'Come on, fall in, Winky Dink!' They took it off the air because some kids would just forget to put their doggone Winky Dink screen on it. When you put a Winky Dink crayon on one of those [TV] screens, it's history."

He attended St. Anne's Catholic grade school in North Minneapolis, where he started taking piano lessons. His first teacher, Sister Margaret, got transferred after his first year. His second piano teacher was Sister Armell. "We called her Sister Arm-smell," Inhofer said in a recent interview. "But myself and another girl, Rose Ammon, were the best students, so the new teacher allowed us to pick what we wanted to do. I said, 'No classical,' and she said, 'Well, I'm going to give you some light classical.' I got stuff like Edvard Grieg. But otherwise, I got to pick popular songs, like 'Cast Your Fate to the Wind' [Vince Guaraldi jazz hit, 1962]. I got books like *Pop Sticks*—it was boogie-woogie. It taught me left-hand stuff. For my eighth-grade recital, I picked a piece called 'The Bumblebee Boogie'—it was the Steve Allen version of 'The Flight of the Bumblebee.' There was one part that I screwed up, and I screwed it up the rest of my life—until last year during Covid. I decided, 'Doggone it, I'm going to fix it.'"

Despite being intrigued by certain songs, Inhofer wasn't really interested in jazz in his early teen years. "I liked it, I enjoyed it, I would memorize stuff, but I wasn't improvising," Inhofer said. "I was learning what was on paper. I did not understand the piano as an emotive instrument at that time."

His Catholic education took him to Crosier Seminary in Onamia, Minnesota, for his first two years of high school. He had attended a symposium in seventh or eighth grade, presented by all the Catholic orders and attended by students from all the area parochial schools. "They would try to indoctrinate them into becoming a priest or a nun or a brother," Inhofer said.

I had my picture taken at one in a little Crosier habit, but for the rest of the day I found a piano over in the corner and I was playing Beatles songs with my friends. We're horsing around, and on the bus on the way home I've got nothing [no brochures] in my bag, just a picture of me in a Crosier habit. This girl, Theresa Connor, says, "Oh, I've got some," because she got everything—priests, nuns, brothers' books—so she gave me a bunch of priest and brothers' stuff, and I take it home and throw it on the dining room table. "Yeah, that's what I did in school today." My dad's looking through it and he sees this Crosier Seminary, and it was like $570 dollars a year including room and board. You just had to pay for some extra stuff. He was worried about me. At that time, I was about 4-foot-9, 93 pounds wet. The next year in high school I'd be going into North High. At that time North High was predominantly a black high school. We'd just had the race riot on Plymouth Avenue. He knew I would go to school and get my ass kicked twice a day— once on the way in and once on the way home. Twice a day, for the rest of my life. So he was interested in this. He brought it up to me and I'm thinking, "Well, he really wants me to go; four years isn't that long." So I agreed to go.

Inhofer said there was one month during the two years at Crosier that he actually wanted to be a priest, because of a sermon delivered by an old priest during one Sunday benediction. "He goes, 'Now, boys, imagine you're on a bus. The bus goes over a cliff. And burns. Wouldn't it be better if you were a priest on that bus?' And for a month I thought, 'Yeah, it would, that would be better'—but that wore off real quick."

The seminary wasn't a great fit for Inhofer, but there was one far-reaching benefit: he met a guitar teacher there. "He teaches me the I-IV-V—the blues chords," Inhofer said. "We start a band called the Silhouettes, the first rock band we've ever had in the seminary. All we had was folk groups. We got the Beatles and the Stones approved for the rec room. We would play these shows, and I would play bass on a six-string electric guitar, and the priest would say, 'We didn't even know you were alive until we saw your fingers moving.'"

It was 1964, when the Beatles and the other British Invasion bands were sweeping the country, and now Inhofer was listening to the radio every chance he got. But his musical education did not begin and end with Beat music from the British Isles. He also had the freedom to visit the seminary's music room and listen to modern composers. "The stuff I got turned on to at the time was what was cool," he said. "I was listening to Edgard Varèse, Charles Ives—ever heard his album with two pianos tuned a quarter-tone apart? Oh, my god. The physical feelings from hearing the same chord being played a quarter-tone apart, and then they start interacting? I mean, come on. Very real physical weirdness. Anyway, that's the stuff I was listening to, this avant-garde classical stuff, because that's what Father Mayer had down there."

Inhofer's band played for the student body once a month. They changed their name from the Silhouettes to The Guys and then went home at the end of the school year. He started another band that summer called the Liberty Three, in which he played lead guitar. When he returned to the seminary in the fall, he switched to lead guitar with The Guys because their lead guitarist had bought an actual bass guitar and wanted to play it. The Guys were asked to play for a sock hop in town and received permission from the prefect to leave the campus for the gig. One small problem: their equipment was inadequate, so they went to the seminary gym and stole the school's PA system, then stole a pickup truck, put their gear in, and drove to town to play the dance. "We make twenty bucks, five bucks apiece—my first paying gig," Inhofer said. "We go back, bring the truck back, go back into the gym to put the speakers back on the wall, we turn on the light in the back room, and there's the head rector, the head guy, sitting in the dark with his dog, waiting for us." As punishment, the band members were put on KP for a month, every Saturday, during which "we'd just sit and listen to the Beatles."

Inhofer found out that the band's drummer was not planning to return to the seminary for his third year, so he decided not to go back either. "I said, 'No band? I'm not going.'"

He transferred to DeLaSalle, the Catholic high school in downtown Minneapolis, for his junior and senior years. "My dad still didn't want me getting my ass kicked twice a day," Inhofer said. "And also, I remember coming home the first summer. Everybody played every intramural sport, so I was playing every sport I'd never played. I was playing football, baseball, hockey, basketball, tennis, everything through the whole year. I went in 4 feet 9 inches, 93 pounds. I came home 5 feet 3 inches, 130 pounds." There, he started playing guitar along with records like *East–West* by the Paul Butterfield Blues Band and *Axis: Bold as Love* by Jimi Hendrix. During his senior year, he met Ron Merchant, the bass player with a local group called the City Strangers. The other members of the band, all students at Minneapolis South High School, were keyboard player Larry Norling and brothers Bob and Dale Strength, sons of country-western recording artist and deejay Texas Bill Strength.

"They were looking for a second guitar and a vocal," Inhofer said. "Ron said, 'Hey, you want to come and audition?' I said, 'Sure.' So I went down and auditioned. And when we got done, Dale said, 'Yeah, what was your name again?' I said, 'Gregg.' He said, 'I don't like that. I'm going to call you Grape.' So for about four years I was Grape. That was my name around town—'Hey, Grape! How are you?' 'Purple. How are you?'"

City Strangers changed their name to Rubberband in January 1968, when Inhofer joined, and began playing heavier rock songs by Hendrix, Cream, and The Who. Then Norling left the band ("the keyboard player wasn't into it"); now a four-piece, the band changed its name again to Flight. They were booked by Jim Donna, the former keyboard player for the Castaways, cowriter of "Liar, Liar," who was running his own booking agency. Rather than attend college in the fall of 1968, Inhofer went all in with his new band. They entered a contest sponsored by film company MGM, competing for a chance to appear in a movie. They recorded a cover version of "Sugar and Spice" by the Cryan Shames, submitted it to Twin Cities rock station KDWB, and were selected to compete in the Midwest finals in Chicago. They also won the opportunity to open a concert at the Minneapolis Armory for a teen idol from India named Sajid Kahn, who starred in the American film—and later NBC TV series—*Maya* and recorded two singles on the Colgems label. Kahn entered the Armory riding an elephant. Flight flew to Chicago in

December for the MGM contest, but their lip-synched version of "Sugar and Spice" lost out to another group.

With that avenue closed, the band was again looking for a new direction. Dale Strength wanted the band to learn the song "Fresh Garbage," the opening track on the debut album by the Los Angeles band Spirit. There was a Wurlitzer electric piano and an upright piano in the basement of the home of their new manager, Joe Budnick, a high school kid who lived with his parents in Minneapolis. Strength suggested a competition between guitarist Inhofer and bassist Merchant to see who could learn the song the fastest. Inhofer was eager to return to the keyboard.

"When I got into high school, I picked up guitar because it was an emotive instrument," Inhofer said. "I could do whatever I wanted to on it. I didn't realize I could do that on piano yet. Ron and I had both taken piano lessons in grade school and could both play our recital piece by memory, but we couldn't really play. Whoever could learn that lick first was going to play piano, and I learned it a split second ahead of Ron. Had I not, I'd probably be a bass player today. Because once I learned one song on piano, well, . . . we might as well add some more. I kept adding more songs and more songs, and then I started writing on piano, which I'd never done before."

With the new instrumentation, it was time for another name change for the band. They became Pepper Fog: "We saw the Jimi Hendrix concert [film] at Monterey, and on the stage were some crates of Pepper Fog, and we said, 'Yeah, that's a good name.'" The band played all over the state, from the Iron Range to Austin, and their experiences on the road perfectly captured that wild, experimental era of rock music.

"We worked with the phony Animals in Minneapolis," Inhofer said. "They had fake accents. Dale's from the south, and the guitar player said [in a southern drawl], 'Hey, you're from Alabama, too? Yeah, dang, that's really good. Well, we gotta go onstage now. We'll see ya later.' He gets onstage. [In heavy British accent] 'Halloo! We'ah the Animals. Eric is sick and cahn't be here, but he sends his luv!'" The last gig on this short

Pepper Fog *(left to right)*: Dale Strength, Bob Strength, Gregg Inhofer, Ron Merchant. Courtesy of Gregg Inhofer.

tour of Minnesota was canceled. "When we got there, there was nobody there but the janitor at a little VFW," Inhofer recalled. "He says, 'Nah, that got canceled a week ago.'"

So Pepper Fog took the promoter to court—and won. The promoter was a young kid named Scott who lived at his parents' house in Willmar, Minnesota. The band first tried going to the house and demanding their money. "Here we are, this bunch of long-haired kids; we're trying to intimidate his parents," Inhofer said. "There was a pie over on the counter and Bob Strength walks over to the pie and cuts himself a piece. These two people were scared to death of us." But they didn't get the money, so they sued Scott. In court, Scott told the judge, "Well, I just don't have the money."

"Scott, it says here that last summer you had a prize head of cattle that won a blue ribbon at the state fair," the judge replied. "What does one of those cattle sell for, Scott? I think you can afford to pay these boys two hundred and fifty dollars." And so he did.

Pepper Fog played a multiband gig in Duluth headlined by the Buchanan Brothers, a studio creation put together by producers Terry Cashman, Tommy West, and Gene Pistilli. They scored two hits in 1969: "Son of a Loving Man" and "Medicine Man." "There was probably half a dozen versions of the Buchanan Brothers going around the country," Inhofer said. "The version we got, the drummer was thirteen, the others were like sixteen, seventeen, and they traveled with their mom and dad in a station wagon pulling a U-Haul. The lead singer was this overweight kid, and he gets up there, and they're the Buchanan Brothers."

In the summer of 1969, Pepper Fog journeyed to Salt Lake City to play a two-week club job with a band billing themselves as the Zombies, the British band that scored a surprise hit earlier that spring with "Time of the Season," a track recorded two years earlier—before they broke up. Inhofer never found out who these purported Zombies were. "We opened, but we didn't have any contact with the band," he said. "They were too cool, too cool for school. They didn't want to talk to any warmup band from Minnesota."

Incorrectly billed as being from New York, Pepper Fog was fired after the first night because they didn't play hits from the current Top 40. They offered to learn every song off the club's jukebox overnight if the owner would keep them on for two weeks, but their pay was cut in half and they were canned after one week. The band took up residence in Salt Lake City for several weeks at a club called the Old Mill, which held weekly jam sessions on Sunday afternoons. Then they landed a three-week job at a club called the Lagoon in a Salt Lake City suburb. Assuming the crowd would want to hear Top 40 material, they bought matching shirts, pants, and ties; after getting a better response to a Jimi Hendrix request, however, they reverted to their more comfortable psychedelic material.

Returning to the Twin Cities, the band members rented an abandoned farm in Plymouth where they could rehearse their increasingly heavy rock material without disturbing anyone. By now they were deeply into psychedelia and progressive rock, a far cry from country hokum like "Tears in My Beer" or "Paper Boy Boogie" recorded by Dale and Bob's father, Texas Bill Strength, who had moved back to the Twin

Cities. "Bill was quite a guy," Inhofer said. "We were recording at Kay Bank. It's one in the morning, we've got our van in the alley, we're loading our gear out, and a pickup truck pulls out. He wants to get through, doesn't want to go the other way. A guy gets out and pulls a gun on Dale. Bill was just walking out—he was playing the Flame [a Minneapolis country bar] and stopped by to see us. He walks over to the guy, takes the gun, puts it to his head, and says, 'You better either use that or get the hell out of here.' The guy got in the van and took off."

When Texas Bill was playing shows at a club in Medicine Lake, he'd park his trailer on the front lawn of Pepper Fog's farmhouse. "He showed up to our place one morning with [country singer] Marvin Rainwater. We're half-asleep when he brings Marvin into the house. We've got this tortoise shell on the wall—that's where we'd hide our stash. Marvin goes, 'Well, this is nice.' He bangs on it and the stash pops out. Bill takes us out and he opens his trunk. He's got hot dogs, hamburgers, buns, relish, pickles, mustard, ketchup, plates, napkins, little salt and pepper shakers, beer, whiskey, vodka, everything for a picnic barbecue. It's 8 o'clock in the fucking morning. So we wake up and start partying with him. Eventually, we barbecue, and friends start showing up, because that's what happened out on the farm. People came out, and we had jam sessions just about every night."

———————

Inhofer talks candidly about the band's drug use during that era, including frequently finishing off an all-night rehearsal by taking LSD and watching the sun come up. Many gigs ended that way, too. "We'd usually drop acid right before the last set, so the colors are just starting to come at the end of the night," he said. "We're in Austin, and Howie Sher is there, and he's got one of these Plymouths with one of the great big, back sloping windows. We're laying in the back, listening to *Beaker Street* [all-night psychedelic show on KAAY Radio from Little Rock]. We all listened to it coming home from gigs, because they were so cool, so great. You'd turn it on and they'd say, 'Yeah . . . Led Zeppelin's got a new album. . . . I'm going to play side one right now. . . . Wow, that was pretty cool. I'm going to play side two.'"

Pepper Fog played several gigs at the Labor Temple in Minneapolis, a venue compared to the Fillmore ballroom in San Francisco. It was booked by promoter/manager David Anthony Wachter and featured the most cutting-edge national and British rock groups, including the Grateful Dead, Jeff Beck, Jethro Tull, Deep Purple, Canned Heat, Procol Harum, Savoy Brown, and Ten Years After, some of whom also played Woodstock in the summer of 1969. In addition to opening for some of those bands, Inhofer and Bob Strength also worked the concession stand at the Labor Temple on concert nights.

Though Pepper Fog did two recording sessions of their original material with engineers Tom Jung and Paul Martinson at Sound 80, they never released an album. Instead, they gigged tirelessly, appearing at the Depot (which became First Avenue) in downtown Minneapolis, the Minnesota State Fair, and at ballrooms and festivals around the region. In February 1972, the band went to the Guthrie Theater to see John McLaughlin and the Mahavishnu Orchestra. Always evolving, Pepper Fog once again transformed its sound, going from underground hard rock to a more jazz–rock fusion direction. They brought in Pat Mackin to play saxophone, but their new sound proved too challenging for much of their fan base. "We broke up," Inhofer said. "All this equipment was coming out, and we didn't have the money to buy it. We signed a contract in blood: 'Okay, we're going to break up for a year. We're going to get jobs and go buy this gear, and then we're going to get back together.' It never happened."

Inhofer began playing in a group called Colla with some of the members of Crow (of "Evil Woman" fame) after that band broke up, including Dave Middlemist on keyboard and guitar, Dick Wiegand on guitar, and Larry Wiegand on bass. Kevin Odegard's old friend Stan Kipper played the drums. "We did that for a few years—that was around the time I was doing the KO [Kevin Odegard] Band, too."

Inhofer then briefly reunited with the Strength brothers and Merchant in a progressive jazz-fusion band called Goldstreet. "We had a summer gig at a place called Mr. Pete's East," Inhofer recalled. "After about two or three weeks, Mr. Pete came to us and said, 'We're just not bringing in the people. Can we negotiate something like you take 60 percent of the till?' 'Sure,' because we're all staying in one room of the hotel, we're rehearsing every day, we're learning everything off the CTI albums with Stanley Turrentine, Freddy Hubbard, George Benson, all this stuff. We learned the whole side of *Tarkus* [Emerson, Lake and Palmer album]. After a couple of weeks of the till, the club owner fired us anyway."

That band evolved into one of Inhofer's most significant aggregations, a jazz-fusion band they dubbed This Oneness. Dale Strength stayed on as lead guitarist, and the rest of the band consisted of Robyn Lee on flute, saxophone, organ, synthesizer, and vocals; Bernie Pershey on drums, percussion, and vocals; and Doug Nelson on bass and vocals. They were playing scattered venues that supported their jazz-fusion style when their fortunes took a wholly unexpected turn.

"Robyn Lee got a call one day from Variety Artists," Inhofer said. "They wanted to know if he was interested in playing organ for this Australian girl that they were rehearsing with in town. He said, 'No, I've got a band. I'm good.' Couple more weeks went by, they called him back. They said, 'Well, could we rent your organ?' This is right before their tour started. He said, 'No.' They called back again a third time, and I guess that's when they asked him if he and maybe some of his band members could do it. So he said, 'I'll bring my guitar player down.' So Dale and Robin went down."

The Australian singer in question was Olivia Newton-John. She had scored a Top 25 single in 1971 with a country-rock version of Bob Dylan's "If Not for You" and after a couple of fallow years had rebounded with "Let Me Be There," a pop and country crossover smash. She came outside to greet the two musicians and noticed Dale Strength's cowboy boots.

"Oh, do you play country music?" she asked.

"Yeah, my dad was a country musician," Strength replied.

"Oh, do you think you could play it better than those fellows?"

Newton-John's producer and guitar player John Farrar had rounded up a group of skilled jazz musicians, but they couldn't play country-rock, which was the core of Newton-John's sound at the time.

"Yeah, we could do it better," Strength said. Farrar fired the other band and hired This Oneness the day before Newton-John's first gig at South Dakota State University in Brookings. As Inhofer recalled:

> We went and got her first album and listened to it once. We went to rehearsal at four o'clock, and we rehearsed for about six hours down at Moon Sound studio [where Prince later recorded the demo for his first single, "Soft and Wet"] with Olivia and John Farrar, who was the main guitar. Dale was the second guitar. They've got charts, easy charts—we're doing fusion music at the time, so it's like, "Yeah, I can do 'Country Roads.'" We go home, pack our bags, and get our gear ready. A Greyhound bus shows up the next morning. We do vocal rehearsal on the bus on the way. She gets a standing ovation and everybody relaxes.

This Oneness toured with Newton-John for two years. One of Inhofer's clearest memories of those days is discovering the British television comedy *Monty Python's Flying Circus* on her tour bus before the show became a hit in the United States. He also recalls the band providing the inspiration for one of Newton-John's biggest hits. "Robyn Lee drank a lot of coffee and he was a hyper guy," Inhofer said. "And he'd be, 'Huh, huh?' And we'd go, 'Robyn, would you just mellow out? Just sit down and mellow out.'"

The expression caught John Farrar's ear.

"Chaps, what is this 'mellow out' that you keep saying to Robyn?" he asked. "What does that mean?"

"I don't know—sit down, take your shoes off, relax," Inhofer replied. Farrar considered the explanation, and then wrote "Have You Never Been Mellow," which became the number-one hit in the nation in March 1975, the same time that *Blood on the Tracks* was topping the album charts. "We told him what it meant, and he goes home and writes a million-dollar hit song," Inhofer said. "What the hell? Why couldn't we do that?"

Though jazz-fusion was Inhofer's first love, he had nothing but good things to say about the experience of performing Newton-John's slick, country-pop-oriented music. When they appeared on the popular

Midnight Special TV show, Newton-John even threw the spotlight on the band for one number. "I'd like to introduce my band, This Oneness, playing their song, 'Please Let the Sun Shine,'" she announced to the national television audience.

"There's isn't anything negative to say about Olivia," Inhofer said. "She's as nice as she always seemed. When we'd go to see her at Hinkley or one of the other casinos . . . we'd buy tickets to go see her, and then we'd go backstage and her handler would bring her down. She'd run down the ramp and give us all a hug. She was very good—a nice person. Very talented. She had very good pitch."

———————

During their three-week stretches between Olivia Newton-John tours, This Oneness continued to do gigs in the Twin Cities—often at the Longhorn in downtown Minneapolis. "We'd spend two weeks rehearsing, then we'd go play a week, and then go back on the road for several weeks," Inhofer said. During those years, Inhofer lived on a farm in Eagan with Bernie Pershey, the Strength brothers, Robyn Lee, and Bob Van Dell, who had replaced Pershey on drums with the Newton-John touring band. Pershey chose not to go on the road at first, and Van Dell was a perfect replacement. "Bob went out on the first couple of tours," Inhofer said. "Bob has got the low voice, so Bob did all the 'Oh, let me be there' vocals. He did it great. Then Bernie came back to join the band, and we took him out, and I regretted it ever since. Because he [Pershey] hated the gig. He would love it now, but he hated the gig, and Bob loved the gig. We should have kept Bob and said, 'Okay, Bernie, we'll be home, then we'll go out and do gigs [as This Oneness], and you'll be here. You can take care of the farm and go do gigs. Have fun.' But unfortunately, it didn't work that way."

Inhofer also sat in with Odegard's KO band when he was available. "Gregg and I had been working together," Odegard said. "We did a benefit together at the Guthrie for the Teen Corps and we were good friends." When Inhofer got the call from Odegard in late December 1974, he was off the road and had no immediate gigs lined up. Odegard told him he needed him for a recording session at Sound 80. "I didn't know it was for a Dylan session—just that it was for a session," Inhofer said. "That was not as common as it later became, as I started to do more commercial work."

In one of Inhofer's previous jobs at Sound 80, he was pounding out vigorous rock 'n' roll on a demo recording for a singer named David Peroni when he heard a rattle in the studio's brand-new Bösendorfer piano. "Finally, Martinson comes out and he looks in there, and one of the bridge saddles had popped," Inhofer said. "It was a $90,000 piano. It was a bad weld. If I wasn't pounding on it, if somebody had been tinkling on it, it might not have happened for years, and they would have said, 'Oh—warranty's over. Bye. Get it fixed yourself.' So I did Herb a favor."

On December 27, 1974, Inhofer headed back to Sound 80 with no idea that he was about to become a part of history.

5

"He's Singing His Song for Me"

KEVIN ODEGARD AND CHRIS WEBER ARRIVED AT SOUND 80 together on December 27, chauffeured by Odegard's girlfriend, Nancy Bundt. "I was not allowed in," she said.

"It was bone-chilling cold," Odegard recalled. "A freezing Minnesota winter night—the temperature was right around zero, before wind chill. So we arrived in full jackets and parkas and unpacked our gear."

Paul Martinson was setting up the room by himself. He'd hoped to have Scott Rivard as his assistant, but Rivard had to leave, so Martinson took on the job of placing baffles and positioning microphones by himself. He was a bit concerned about not having help, but he'd worked with David Zimmerman before and knew he'd been chosen to record the session because of Zimmerman's faith in him. "Knowing Kevin and Gregg, and having worked a lot with Peterson and Berg, I was able to go into it with reasonable confidence," Martinson was quoted in Andy Gill and Odegard's 2005 book *A Simple Twist of Fate*. "I figured that once we had set up the session, I wouldn't have to change very much, because it would stay the same, both players and equipment."

Gregg Inhofer was next to arrive, still under the impression that he was there for an ordinary commercial session. He walked into the studio and spotted Martinson right away. "I did a bunch of work with Paul," Inhofer said. "His pants were always halfway down his ass." Odegard then told Inhofer the secret he'd been keeping: they were doing a Bob Dylan recording session.

"Really?" Inhofer said. "You didn't tell me it was Bob Dylan. God."

When Dylan arrived, Odegard met him and shook his hand—receiving what Odegard described as Dylan's trademark limp handshake. Odegard recalled Dylan as being "chatty, friendly, and engaging—comfortable to be with." Inhofer could tell right away that Dylan had a cold. "He pretty much kept to himself," Inhofer said. "He kind of sat over on the side. He kept his coat on and just sat there."

As the other musicians arrived, each had their own moment of recognition and adjustment as they dealt with the presence of rock's most reclusive superstar. When Berg made his way from the icy parking lot into the studio, Dylan was getting coffee from a vending machine in the breakroom down the hall with his son, Jakob, and David's son, Seth, in tow. "I walk in the studio, and there's Bob just standing in the doorway with, I remember, a leather jacket I think he had on," Berg said. "Talk about surreal. You know, here he is, standing in front of me." There was no acknowledgment on either Dylan's or Berg's part that they had both grown up in Hibbing. "Not one bit," Berg said. "Bob does not ever do small talk, that I've ever heard. So it was only about the music, and hardly much about that at all."

"I came into the studio with my electric bass over my shoulder, and I'm walkin' my upright bass in," Billy Peterson said. "I showed up, and there he was—hair all up here, you know? So I look around the room and I backed out through the door. David was standing back by the door into Studio A and the control room. I said, 'Okay David, what the hell's going on? There's your very famous brother sitting in the studio there. What are we doing?' He said, 'I couldn't tell you he was going to be here.' I had an attitude: 'Oh yeah, this shit's gonna work. You're going to throw our rhythm section behind your famous brother.'"

———

The musicians needed some time for their instruments—and their bodies—to warm up. "Any players who work in Minneapolis know that there's gotta be a warmup time for the instruments—session or gig," Berg said. "It's just so cold. In fact, sometimes you can break a drumhead, even a plastic drumhead, by bringing it in from the cold and whacking it. So you kinda warm up and loosen up, and here's Bob. You want to be at your very best, of course. So it was a crazy night."

In a 2016 interview, Weber had a clear recollection of his introduction to Dylan. After greeting Peterson, Berg, and Inhofer, Dylan walked over to Weber and stuck out his hand.

"Hi, I'm Bob Dylan."

Weber recalled replying similarly, with a smirk: "Hi, I'm Chris Weber." Dylan looked at Weber with a quizzical expression, but Weber immediately got down to business. "I brought that vintage guitar that you were asking about."

"Oh yeah, you got the—oh, okay," Dylan said. "Let's take a look at that." They were standing next to the vocal booth, which Weber described as looking like two old-school phone booths—the kind Superman would change clothes in—just big enough for two chairs and a microphone, where the singer could record his voice, glassed in from the band. Weber opened the guitar case and pulled out the Martin. Dylan must have felt as though he had been reunited with the instrument on which he'd composed most of the album.

"Oh God, that's beautiful," he said.

"Yeah," Weber replied. Dylan held the instrument and tried to listen to its tone as he played it, but the other musicians in the room were setting up and tuning their instruments.

"You could take it in there, and you'd be able to hear it," Weber said, motioning to the vocal booth. Dylan nudged Weber with his right elbow.

"Yeah, let's do that."

Dylan brought a second guitar into the vocal booth, then sat down opposite Weber and closed the door. Weber's heart was already racing at the thrill of meeting his idol, and he became even more excited as they sat knee to knee with each other in the small space.

"Do you play?" Dylan asked.

"Sure, I've played all my life."

"Great. Well, do you write anything?"

"Yeah, I've written some things."

"Good. Why don't you play me something you wrote on that guitar, and I can sit in front of it and I can hear what it really sounds like."

Not knowing what Dylan had in mind, he played a fingerpicking tune called "A-Rag," which he described as a fun, light tune. It lasted just over a minute.

"Whoa, you play well," Dylan said.

"Thanks."

"Do you write any words?"

"Yeah, I've written some words," Weber said, feeling like a kid with a notepad on the streets of Elizabethan London when Shakespeare walks by and asks if he's writing poetry. But Weber recalled that Dylan was being very nice to him, speaking with a twinkle in his eye—as if to say he knew how intimidating the situation was and he was sympathetic.

"Come on, sing me some words," Dylan said.

Weber sang a song he wrote called "Come on Home with Me," about a troubadour on the road, looking in the front row for the girl he was going to pick up and take back to the hotel to keep him warm: "Come on home with me / I don't need to know your name / I don't need to know your game / Just spend the night with me." Dylan listened to the whole song.

"That's a nice tune," he said. "Linda Ronstadt should do that."

Of course, Weber was thinking, "Yeah, Bob, make the call," but that was not the matter at hand. Dylan was there to record his own songs and finish his album.

"Listen, do me a favor," Dylan said. "Learn this tune here; let me teach you this tune. I'm gonna go visit with my boys in the breakroom. Come and get me when [the other musicians] know the tune."

The song was "Idiot Wind," which opens with an unusual chord change from C minor to D. Dylan played it, Weber repeated it, and then Dylan went back to the first chord.

"What's the name of that chord?" Dylan asked.

"C minor?"

"Yeah, the C minor." Years later, Weber was still not sure whether Dylan was testing his knowledge, or whether he really didn't know the name of the chord. It seems likely that it was a test; Odegard marveled at Dylan's ability throughout the sessions to instantly transpose songs into different keys.

"But it was pretty clear, at least at that point in his life, and my life, I was a better player, and he was acknowledging that," Weber said. It also became clear that this was not going to be a repeat of the failed New York band sessions, where Dylan did not try to help the musicians learn the songs and Phil Ramone declined to intervene. At Sound 80, Dylan led Weber through the changes chord by chord—in standard tuning.

"No Joni Mitchell [open tuning] shenanigans," Odegard recalled:

David was the architect of getting rid of the tunings. They would be harder to follow in the studio. Your bass player would wonder, "What the hell is that?" If you're a good musician, a studio cat, even with a capo you can follow in standard tuning. How do you follow Joni Mitchell through a song? She really was like Bob; she was her own producer. I think the tunings were his Achilles heel—once he let them go, in a Zen way, this idea that it needed to be a song cycle, a rock opera, a folk opera, once he let that go, he was free to get back to the basics. He never even used a capo. He was at the top of his form. What I saw in our session was a guitar master, demonstrating, plucking, strumming, picking, and overdubbing two guitars, a mandolin, an organ, and harmonica. He was just in a zone with his home boys in Minnesota that, evidently, he couldn't find in New York and elsewhere. I believe Bob wasn't fully baked on the material in New York. The session musicians there being more rigid than we were. They could not run with the football.

Unlike New York, there was actual give-and-take with the Minnesota musicians. While teaching "Idiot Wind" to Weber, Dylan played an A minor over the lyric about taking Gray's wife to Italy, but Weber heard it as an A minor 7th.

"Whoa, wait a minute; what'd you do there?" Dylan asked.

"You played an A minor 7th there, right?" Weber said.

"No, I didn't. I played an A minor. But I like that A minor 7; leave that in there."

Ever afterward, Weber liked to tell people he'd changed a chord in a Bob Dylan song. Such moments appealed to Dylan's desire for spontaneity; as always with Dylan, the moment was everything. His songs could change a dozen different ways before and after they were recorded, but he put down on tape what he liked right now, with a minimum of rehearsing. For this session he wanted the band to know the song before the tape started rolling, so he wouldn't have to do a lot of retakes.

"Chris learned the song and then Bob would sit alone in the vocal booth and polish the lyrics," Odegard said. "He would use message slips, put it back and forth, and rearrange the verses up and down and back and forth, and then once he had done that and he looked at it, he had an amazing ability to memorize it. To this day, Bob Dylan gets onstage and sings hundreds and hundreds of his songs just from memory. The man's got a photographic memory."

As Weber demonstrated the chording to "Idiot Wind," it began to dawn on the rest of the musicians that this was a serious Bob Dylan recording session. "I thought for a minute we may be just doing a little demo thing, and he may want to listen to something, a tune that we interpreted in a different way," Berg said. "But it was the real deal, so it was surreal, to say the least." Berg quickly figured out the rhythm pattern he would play on the song. Peterson jotted down a chord chart for himself. Inhofer initially thought he'd be playing Hammond organ on the tune, but it was an instrument he didn't own or have much experience with. Dylan showed him the part he wanted played but then decided to play it himself as an overdub.

"You play the piano," he said to Inhofer.

Odegard was not asked to play on "Idiot Wind," and Weber assumed his services were no longer needed either. It would have been enough for him to sit in the control booth and watch Dylan record. "He was totally a Dylan fan," Vanessa Weber said. "When he first heard him, each of us were in agreement that this guy cannot sing, and was not that great a player, but boy, can he write words. 'Tambourine Man,' Peter, Paul and Mary, so many songs out there played by other people.... Once we started listening to his words, that was it. Chris had him firmly on the pedestal."

When Dylan spotted Weber behind the glass in the booth with

Martinson, he gave him an odd look, so Weber went out into the studio and asked if it would be all right if he stayed around to watch the session. "No, man, I need you to play guitar," Dylan said. They set up a mike for Weber, who played the Martin 00-42 he'd brought for Dylan.

"Chris is the only musician that Bob Dylan hired," Vanessa Weber said. "The others were picked out by David. Dylan threw him on the stage."

Odegard described Sound 80's Studio A—which still exists, though it's not a commercial studio anymore—as an L-shaped room off the main hallway and foyer, with a glassed-in sound booth in the corner. "There are great, wonderful studio monitors inside," Odegard said. "There's a huge board and a vocal booth directly opposite from the mixing booth. It's laid out perfectly so you can see everything and you can hear everything. It had state-of-the-art mics, U87s everywhere, coming out of your ears. Martinson knew every piece of gear, and he would say, 'Put a U87 out here and a condenser over there for the guitars, and mic the drums this way.' And once he was set up for the first session, we just left it that way. Nobody else, fortunately, was in there all weekend."

"We were all pretty much in the same room," Inhofer said. "Drums behind plexiglass there, and Billy direct. I was just sitting there and Bob was right out in the room. Paul took command of the session because David Zimmerman, the producer, is not a music producer per se. I mean, I am not criticizing him at all, but that's not his gig. He was there to help facilitate Bob doing the songs. But Paul took command. He said, 'This is what we're going to do, and we're going to put this here and we're going to do that there.'"

"I didn't have a guitar out at that point," Odegard recalled. "I had my Martin in its case. So I was an observer and I was in the sound booth watching this whole thing. It was tough to get over that first C minor chord—it was dissonant, awkward, tough on the ears—but eventually Berg and Peterson figured it out, and Inhofer was just all over it right away. Chris massaged it a little bit there in the vocal booth and got the arrangement around to the point where the attack was quite startling: 'Someone's got it in for me!' and it was just perfect on that tape. I think we did seven or eight takes on that. They jumped right into it, and by the time we really got kind of warmed up in the room as a band, it was sounding really, really good, and Bob started to relax a little bit. By the seventh or eighth take, I'm not sure which it was, it was perfect, and very little was done after that."

Odegard was thrilled with the song because it seemed to recapture some of the old spite and vitriol of classics like "Positively Fourth Street" and "Like a Rolling Stone." For whatever reason, Dylan was now spitting out the lyrics with a vengeance he had not shown during the more laid-back versions cut in New York.

"I think we locked in on a tempo pretty early," Berg said. "Because in those days, Bob was dense with his lyrics, and so passionate. I always liked to kinda trot the tempo back a little bit, if possible, because you don't want to force the singer to be just rattling the lyrics off and not able to express these emotions that he's got. With Billy on bass, Billy and I had done all this stuff together, so we really could play time together. And Gregg and the rest of the guys, everybody just sorta felt it, you know, at that tempo."

Berg was also thinking about how to interpret the lyrics with subtle embellishments that would not attract attention to himself but rather augment the story being told. "When he said, 'I shot a man named [Gray],' there was an instant wham on the middle of the snare drum, and that was spontaneous," Berg said. "I didn't know the lyrics that well, and we weren't looking at any lyric sheets or anything. So some of that was just in response. And I tried to listen as hard as I could to his lyrics and his direction and his dynamics and his phrasing—all those things that good studio players do."

Odegard, listening in the control booth, was particularly impressed with that touch.

"Before he's done saying the word 'shot,' [Berg was] on that snare. And [he] stuck it. That's true. Before he's done with the word—that's how fast [he] responded."

Berg even brought a little piece of Hibbing, Minnesota, to the official recording of "Idiot Wind." "I had an old [Zildjian] K ride cymbal that I got out of the basement of Crippa Music in Hibbing," Berg said. "It was a used cymbal; I think it had a crack in the edge or something.

And that's what I think Billy and I and the rest of the band got into, you know, when we did 'Idiot Wind.' It was just such an angry piece of music, that we just brought out our jazz feel and our own angst. The attitude was there, and that cymbal helped that track."

"These things were all baptism by fire," Peterson said. "Dylan was a point A to point B performer. No punch [splicing to replace a mistake]. Come on, we're gonna do this straight through, right? So we were all of that same mindset—old school. The greatest generation's school. The way Frank Sinatra did it; the way Jeanne did it, my mom. Performance level, you know? You start the song and you finish it. You don't think about a punch; you have continuity."

Odegard said the session was originally planned for just the new version of "Idiot Wind." "He wanted it to have more edge," Odegard said. "That was it. But it went so well, we did seven takes. It kept getting better and better. Bill Berg really got into the pocket, and it drove Dylan crazy, it drove him nuts. He was wild with creativity."

After the final take, Dylan knew he had a much more urgent version of the song, but there were parts he wanted to add. He overdubbed the organ part he'd initially asked Inhofer to play, while Inhofer overdubbed a piano part. "It was Bob playing the Hammond on 'Idiot Wind' and me playing the piano, and we're the only ones in the studio," Inhofer recalled. "I have to say that I looked over and went 'Wow. I'm doing an overdub with Bob Dylan. Son of a bitch!'"

"It was disbelief," Odegard said. "It was suspension of belief because, like being in a movie, it was surreal."

Berg initially had to fight off the same sense of amazement. "When you first put your headphones on, and here's Bob's voice coming through your headphones, that was something right there," he said. "So I had to, for a minute, pinch myself and say, 'Okay, get back on the drums now. You gotta play. You gotta listen to what Billy's doing, you gotta listen to what Gregg's doing, you gotta listen to what Bob's doing.' Because we had a lot of players, and you can't fill up every single eighth note, sixteenth note. You gotta leave a little air. So I was thinking of that all along."

"You know when you're under the gun to do something like that,"

Peterson said. "I don't know if my mind said, 'Whoa, this is really fun,' because you have a job to do. I think I was going, 'Wow, this is really happening.' I'm sitting here like this, and he's looking at me, we're playing, right? And this is going down because we're all recorded at the same time in the same rooms in those days. Inhofer'd be over on the B3, and all the guys were over here, so we were all in the same room. I don't think I said, 'Well, this is a ball.' When you're in that thing in the moment, you do the best job you can to showcase the music as it's going down. When I'm doing that kind of performing, my mind is not totally consumed with, 'Hey, this is really fun, cool.' That's not why I'm hired."

Peterson had heard horror stories about Dylan being hell on studio musicians but was pleased to see another side of Bob Dylan. "It wasn't like we were being subservient," Peterson said.

> Bob was, like, just hanging out, man, one of the cats. He was looking to get bailed out of a record he didn't dig. We were like family, and he was like a choir boy. He wasn't ordering us around; he was looking for input. He was getting divorced. The whole record was about his breakup. It was a family gathering. Jakob was running around the studio, Bob was babysitting. Bob's strong point, which was kind of surprising to me, was his openness to our creativity. When you get a big celebrity star like that coming through, they usually have a certain thing in their mind that they want to hear out of you. They'll say, "Hey, you know this part? None of that." So the door was open, as far as creativity. And he asked, after these takes, "Do you think you had it?" I think they all felt great. Every take we did felt great. Originally, we didn't know what he wanted to do. I think he didn't know what he wanted to do. He didn't know we could play. Then he went, "Holy shit, these guys are bringing something to the party."

Things were going well on both sides of the glass. Once Martinson figured out the proper balance between the instruments and Dylan's voice, he felt he had achieved the optimum rough mix, as he told Gill and Odegard later. "At Sound 80, we were taught to start mixing immediately on the first run-through," Martinson said. He explained that many clients didn't have a lot of time or money to spend in the studio recording their two songs, so the engineers mixed straight to two-track and gave the mix to the mastering engineer. It also gave the artists a good feel for how the end product would sound when they listened to the playback. When Dylan went into the control room to listen to "Idiot Wind," he told Martinson, "You have a nice way of picking things up here." That relaxed the engineer, who said to himself, "Oh, good, he likes it. We're going to do some pretty good work here."

If the original plan was to re-record "Idiot Wind" and call it a night, that plan was discarded when it became clear that the musicians in the studio were fully capable of doing anything Dylan wanted. He asked the band to learn the chord changes to one of the album's most gentle songs, "You're a Big Girl Now."

Unfortunately for Peterson, the session had already taken up all the time he had to spare. Natural Life was playing their regular Friday night gig at the Longhorn in downtown Minneapolis, and saxophonist Bob Rockwell would not accept any excuses for missing or being late for a gig. Peterson understood his obligation and told Dylan he had to leave. "It was just me being twenty-three years old and having this steady gig that people depended on me," he said. "Dylan said, 'God, wish we could come down and hear you guys.' He was a big Bohemian mofo. Hung out with Monk and all those guys. I remember him saying, 'I'm going to come down and hear you.' And I said, 'Yeah, Bob, you're not going to get mauled by fans.' He never did, of course. He was real nice in letting me go."

"I know he wanted to stay, but he had to get to the gig because of Rockwell," Odegard said. "I think he [Rockwell] confronted him later and said, 'I don't care who you're recording with. You're going to show up for your gig on time. This is your gig here.'"

"Do I regret leaving the Dylan session to go play with Bob Rockwell and those guys?" Peterson asked in retrospect. "No, because it left an endearing taste in everybody's mouth that I was gone and Dylan gave me the nod and said, 'No, go ahead, man.' I couldn't mess with those guys. It was all original material; I couldn't call Gordy Johnson and say, 'Gordy, go sub for me.'"

Peterson's absence did not deter Dylan from taking a crack at "You're a Big Girl Now." He had recorded several takes of the song in New York, some solo and some with Tony Brown on bass. The version that was scheduled for release included Brown, as well as Paul Griffin on organ and an overdubbed steel guitar by Buddy Cage. At Sound 80, Dylan did two takes of the song on guitar and harmonica with Weber on second guitar, Berg on drums, and Inhofer on piano. Then he added extra guitar parts. "Bob picked up an acoustic guitar and overdubbed flamenco leads on that one," Odegard said. "I think he did two passes, and it was done in the can—two songs done. He was only intending to do one song, so the second song that night was a bonus for all of us."

"He did like one thing I did," Inhofer said. "At the end of 'You're a Big Girl Now,' I played a third in the bass on the last chord. He said, 'Hey, what's that? Ooh, I like that, keep that in.'"

"Other than ['Idiot Wind'], I would say there would be a run-through of the first verse and then one, maybe two takes," Odegard said. "That was all it took for 'You're a Big Girl Now,' and then later on, they became fewer and fewer takes, because Bob got more and more comfortable."

———————

Everyone was feeling good about the session when it broke up—perhaps Berg more than any of the others, because of the unspoken Hibbing connection:

Being the Grain Belt, Bible Belt, we're simple, a good bunch of people, and we do good work. The fact that he's Bob, recording in his home state: we were all a little starstruck. It wasn't just like, "Here's another artist." This was a big deal. As much as the town of Hibbing didn't go out of their way to support Bob in the early years, maybe Minneapolis did—the Triangle Bar, all that stuff, before moving east. The fact that our state was the home for such a musical genius like Bob, once he came back, we wanted to do him proud, and Dave, too. Intrinsically, I believed that, because we'd gone to the same high school, the same pizza places, all things Iron Range, whether he'd had all the success or not, there was a connection: "Yep, I know your family, your dad, your mom, your brother." You look to the town fathers as guiding forces in your life. His dad, Abe Zimmerman, was one of the nicest men. My mom knew Beatty. She was always very sweet to us: "Come on in, you guys rehearse down in the basement." There was just such a warmth and inclusion. The fact that ten years later I'm in the studio with Bob, I felt this couldn't be more special. I was so honored in a way to be called to do this work.

"I remember that there was this great presence in the room," Odegard said. "He had a vibe. Let's just say he had a tremendous aura, and it was a wonderful, benevolent aura to be around. I don't know whether Robert Allen Zimmerman is actually Bob Dylan the movie star or not, but there's this vessel of heavenly lyrics and music that pours out of this man's soul. Whether or not Robert Zimmerman is attached to it, I'm not sure, but he was about halfway between those two personalities for these two sessions. He was in Minnesota, with his guard down a little bit, looking to make some really great music again. You could tell all that stuff by his stance. As the sessions went by, he became happier and happier with the results and kept going."

Even though he hadn't been asked to play, Odegard was so pumped up that he immediately violated David Zimmerman's non-disclosure policy. "David said, 'Don't call anybody from the studio'—a rule which I broke right away," Odegard said. "I called my girlfriend, Nancy Bundt, trying to get her over there with the camera, but it wasn't meant to be. David put the hammer down and said, 'No cameras.'" Everyone present adhered to that edict, which is why there are no photos of the Dylan recording sessions at Sound 80. But it was impossible for the musicians to keep the experience to themselves. Chris Weber called Vanessa immediately after they finished. She had planned to come pick him up when the session was over, but he said she didn't have to come.

"I've got a ride home," he told her. "It was a Bob Dylan session."

Vanessa had to ask him if he'd really said it was Bob Dylan. Inhofer, meanwhile, managed to contain his enthusiasm. He'd enjoyed the session, but he wasn't overwhelmed by Dylan's presence. "I guess I wasn't starstruck," he said. "Our band was out with Olivia Newton-John at the time, so we were meeting lots of people. We opened for Don Rickles, the Smothers Brothers, and Norm Crosby in Vegas. It's not like I got on the phone and said, 'Hey, man, I just did a session with Dylan.' I went back to the farm. 'Who was the session with?' 'Bob Dylan.' 'Yeah, cool. Wanna listen to the new Weather Report album?'"

Odegard didn't know exactly how to process the experience. "It was almost like I couldn't pick up the phone because nobody would believe me," he said. "I've gone through my whole life with better guitar players really not liking me. They see me play guitar and they go, 'So you were really in that room, huh?' So, yeah, it was like a movie."

The movie was about to get a whole lot better.

"We were done," Odegard said. "We knew we were done. We went back to our mundane lives wondering how we were going to explain this to our relatives, who would believe us. Then I get back from [a railroad shift] and the phone's ringing. I pick it up and it's David again. He said, 'Well, Bob is pretty happy and wants to get together again Monday night. And bring your guitar.' It was like, for a musician, as if you met God himself, or herself, and then the phone rang and it was going to happen again. At that point we felt a great brotherhood among the six Minneapolis musicians, which has lasted to this day."

Monday morning, a budding mandolin virtuoso named Peter Ostroushko left his West Bank apartment for the first time in days and walked across the University of Minnesota campus to the Podium guitar shop. He had contracted pneumonia and had been battling a fever but was feeling restless at being cooped up in his apartment. He decided to visit his friend and frequent musical collaborator, banjo player Jim Tordoff, who was refretting one of Ostroushko's mandolins in the Podium's basement repair shop. When Ostroushko walked in, Tordoff gave him a sly smile and asked if he'd seen the shop's owner, Chris Weber.

"I just got here. I haven't seen him."

"Well, when you do, he's going to talk your ear off about something that happened Friday night." A few minutes later, Weber came down the stairs.

"You'll never guess what happened to me," Weber beamed. "I recorded with Bob Dylan at Sound 80, and he says they're going to do it again tonight. They asked me to come back."

Ostroushko was understandably awed. "I would have been shitting my pants," Ostroushko said years later about his reaction to Weber's astounding opportunity to play with Dylan. He could remember listening with his older brother to "Like a Rolling Stone" on the radio ten years earlier, when he was just eleven years old, and being captivated. "Once we got into Dylan, life wasn't the same after that."

Tordoff couldn't resist asking Weber to be included on the second session. "Well, you tell Dylan if he needs a banjo player or a mandolin or fiddle player to give us a call," Tordoff said.

"Okay, I'll do it," Weber agreed. As if that were likely to happen. Outside of the regulars who'd seen him play mandolin, fiddle, and guitar at the folk clubs in the university's West Bank neighborhood, Ostroushko's profile was negligible. He was just twenty-one years old and had never set foot in a recording studio.

His fever was spiking. Ostroushko returned to his apartment and went back to bed.

6

"Every One of Them Words Rang True"

KEVIN ODEGARD DIDN'T THINK HIS CHANCES TO RECORD WITH Dylan were very good, even though he'd been called back. When he walked into Studio A at Sound 80 at 5 p.m., Monday, December 30, he discovered that Paul Martinson had set up an extra chair and mic on the floor. Out of loyalty to his friend, Gregg Inhofer had asked David Zimmerman if it would be possible to get Odegard a chance to play on one of the tracks that night. "After all," Inhofer said, "Kevin got me the gig." Zimmerman made no promises, but he too was looking out for his friend Kevin. As the second session began, Odegard was placed directly to the left of Dylan. He took his Martin D-28 out of its case and waited with eager anticipation for whatever he might be asked to do.

Despite David Zimmerman's firm admonition to the musicians (all of whom happily returned for the second night) that they were not to let the word out about the secret Dylan sessions, there were several more visitors to the studio on Monday, including Vanessa Weber, pregnant with her and Chris's first child. "I did go the second night," she said. "Dylan hadn't brought his harmonicas, so Chris asked me to go to the store and bring all different keys of harmonicas. Stupidly, I didn't grab all the sheet music we had of Dylan and have him sign it. When I came into the studio, he was sitting in the chair. He stood up and shook my hand. He was very quiet but very nice. I sat around for a while and watched, but I was very evident wherever I was. I did meet him, and it was fun. They just clicked, like they'd been rehearsing for years."

More spectators would arrive later.

As on the previous evening, Dylan introduced a new song to Weber, who then taught it to the band. It was the six-minute story song "Tangled Up in Blue"—destined to become a classic but still searching for a definitive arrangement. The open D tuning (capoed up a full step to E) version of the song, recorded three months earlier in New York, was abandoned. Dylan had the Martin 00-42 in standard tuning, and his intention was to record the song in G. The band did a quick run-through, after which Dylan looked around him expectantly. He turned his penetrating stare on the guitarist sitting immediately to his left, Kevin Odegard—like a razor, Odegard recalled. "Daggers through my head, right? Looking right at me."

"Well?" Dylan asked. "What did you think?"

"It's passable."

"Passable?" Dylan said. "What does that mean?"

Odegard felt his heart sink. He was afraid his "passable" comment was going to earn him a quick exit before he'd ever get a chance to record a note. The song's lyric was about to come true: one day the axe just fell. Yet to Odegard's ears the song lacked something.

"It was good," Odegard said, recalling his initial reaction to the song. "It was plenty good, and the story was great and the lyrics were wonderful, switching from first to second to third person, all these characters intermingling and interacting, and it was a lot of fun, but I found myself drifting about halfway through." The version of "Tangled Up in Blue" in G was "just another album cut," as far as Odegard was concerned. "It was just something that would go between other songs."

The mood in the room on that second night had been comfortable. It wasn't Dylan the superstar in the studio with them, but Bob from the Iron Range, enjoying the company and the contributions of these like-minded Minnesotans, who had already proven themselves eminently capable of interpreting and delivering on his creative ideas.

"And I forgot where I was," Odegard admitted. "I forgot who I was talking to. I was just in a room with a bunch of musicians. Bob was relaxed at that point, and the vibe was pretty even, pretty steady, and so I just blurted out, 'Well, it's passable.' There are differences in the keys;

they have different personalities. The folk idiom is around a C or a G. Now, when you get up to A, you're getting into some rock 'n' roll shuffle. You're getting into some edgy stuff. So I thought, 'Edge, edge—let's move it up to A.' But I forgot who I was with—that I was in a room with this guy who had taken the world by storm."

Rather than do what many unknown guitar players would have done in his situation—offer up some mindless flattery so he could remain on the session—he chose to expand on his critique. "Well, you know, it's good, but I think it should be in a higher key," Odegard told Dylan. "I think it would be more exciting, have more energy. You'd be reaching for the notes, and it would play better in the key of A." Then he waited to be told to pack up his guitar and leave.

After a long, agonizing pause, Dylan finally spoke: "Okay, let's try it."

Odegard and Weber capoed up two frets, but Dylan went without a capo, instead transposing the chords from G to A in his head.

"So [Dylan] raised his hand, and he gave the sign, you know, like we hear on *Nashville Skyline*—'Is it rolling, Bob?' [Bob Johnston, Dylan's then-producer]," Odegard said. "With Bob, it's rolling and there's no rehearsal or little rehearsal, and if it works, that's great. He's going to move on. So it's very much a live situation with Bob in the studio. Martinson knew that right away. He was huddled with David Zimmerman in the booth, and they were whispering in each other's ear. David, I'm sure, is telling him this whole time, 'Just roll, just keep rolling, something might happen, just keep rolling,' and Martinson did. Paul was already rolling. Paul said, 'Yeah, let's just do it.' Bob said 'Okay, count it off, Bill [Berg].' And those six minutes—as one of my daughters has told me since—[were] the defining moment of my life. Before or since. I wish it weren't so, but it is."

This signature song from the album included chronological and geographic jumps over seven densely packed verses and lasted five minutes and forty-five seconds. It was still essentially acoustic, but the band continued to heighten the drama as they fed off each other's growing confidence and Dylan's stunning vocal urgency. "By the time the second verse rolls around, Chris is up here on his twelve-string

Martin, doing [licks high up the neck]," Odegard said. "One by one, the musicians jumped on that trend, and that became the most exciting six minutes."

"I listen to it now, and that's got a sense of urgency, that track," Peterson said. "Berg and I were intense all the way through that thing. I'm playing all these melodic lines on the bass and Dylan didn't give me the fisheye once: 'Go ahead, motherfucker!'"

Inhofer does not recall Weber teaching him the chords to "Tangled Up in Blue." Dylan had scrawled the chords to the song in the margin of a newspaper, handed them to Inhofer, and said, "Here's the chords to the next song." Inhofer—the jazz-fusion fan—played the new song with ease but not disrespect. "Just because I wasn't into three-chord music didn't mean I didn't try my best to play it as well as I could," Inhofer said. "I was not cavalier. I wasn't egotistical about it, going, 'Pssh. Yeah, I can play three chords.' No. It was like, I was serious. It was Dylan."

Odegard was not told specifically what to play, so he relied on his own sense of the song and his memory of riffs he liked. He quickly settled on a blues-related acoustic lick played by Terry Garthwaite of Joy of Cooking on a song called "Midnight Blues." "I wanted to put a little something special on the front end, and I sped it up," he said. "This was a very slow lick on the original record, and I lifted it whole cloth and played it on the opening notes and at the beginning of every verse of 'Tangled Up in Blue.' One take. I have never before or since played like that. For those six minutes I was pretty good."

His guitar part is difficult to distinguish in the originally released version of "Tangled Up in Blue," which is actually the safety mix Martinson made during the song's only full take in A. On the 2018 box set of the sessions, *More Blood, More Tracks*, Odegard's playing is clearly audible in the left channel. Dylan was going to mix the tracks immediately after the Monday session, but when he heard Martinson's safety mix, he decided that was the way he wanted the song to sound. "They used to do a thing called safety masters, which is a flying mix on the run as the shit was going down, direct to two-track," Peterson said. "'Tangled Up in Blue' was a Paul Martinson safety master. That's the truth. Paul Martinson was a freak and had unbelievable talent. His nickname was Two—he'd always say, 'Track Two.' Real emphatic about it. Dylan couldn't remix it any better than the stuff Paul had done on the fly. In my head, that proved what a freak Paul Martinson was."

When the song came to an end, every musician in the room, including Dylan, paused several moments without speaking to appreciate the performance they'd just been part of. Years later, the Minneapolis musicians will quickly agree that of the five songs recorded during the two sessions, "Tangled Up in Blue" is the one they immediately knew was special.

"We were transported," Odegard said. "We rocketed into the fourth dimension. We were all off the ground about two feet for the entire six minutes of that song. It could have been six years. When you're transported into another dimension, time goes away and space is all relative. When we landed at the end of that harmonica solo, we glanced at each other briefly, looked at the floor to make sure our feet were still on it. There was a great silence that came over the room and it lasted a while, because you couldn't say anything after that. The thoughts that were rolling through my head had to do with 'Gee, if I ever have kids or grandkids, this is the moment I'm going to tell them about my music career.' That's what I was actually thinking at that point. This is the moment."

———————

After "Tangled Up in Blue," the musicians took a break. "There was nothing else we could do," Odegard said. "It was very powerful. It was spiritual. We were uplifted. Everything beyond that point was going to be gravy. We knew it. The vibe was pleasant. I didn't care if I never played a guitar again. For the rest of my life, that made me fulfilled right there. So we took a break."

Dylan went to the vending machine for more coffee. Odegard ran across the street to Skol Liquors to get a carton of milk for Jakob. Weber went out into the hall to call Peter Ostroushko and Jim Tordoff, because Dylan had asked him if he knew a mandolin player. Before Weber could reach Ostroushko, Dylan had returned to the studio and the musicians were already working on the next song—the sprawling, melodramatic "Lily, Rosemary and the Jack of Hearts."

"I left the studio," Weber said. "No cell phones at that time. So I walk out of the studio and use the phone in the hallway. The door closed and I'm calling these guys to come over—all prearranged, of course. And as I walk out the door, the door closes, the red light goes on—'Do Not Enter; Recording in Session.' And in that short time, Bob had gone over to Gregg and Bill and Billy and taught them the basic three chords to 'Lily, Rosemary and the Jack of Hearts.'"

Dylan had attempted two solo takes of the song on the first night of the New York sessions, getting a complete version of the nine-minute-forty-five-second song on the second try. He never did attempt a version with the full Deliverance band in New York. The solo take was scheduled for inclusion on *Blood on the Tracks*, but Dylan's growing appreciation for his Minneapolis sidemen had apparently convinced him that he could record a better version with this band.

"David came out of the booth and he looked at the guys that were still there," Odegard said. "I was just done—I didn't want to play anymore. And David said to Berg and Peterson in particular, 'So hey, you guys, here's how it is. This is a long song. You might think it's done, but it's not. Just keep playing, because it's not done. This is like a nine-minute song. So just keep on playing.' Bob started playing a few notes. He said, 'Yeah, okay, well, let's just get into it,' and they played it. There was only one take of that song."

"His brother comes through the studio door and he comes up to me," Peterson recalled. "He says, 'Billy, when you think this song is done, it's not done.' I just keep playing and I think, 'That's all the advice you got for me?'"

The key to the Minneapolis version is Berg's propulsive drumming with his brushes. Dylan's solo version meanders along like many story songs in the folk tradition, but with the band behind him the song has the steady hum of a locomotive hurtling down the tracks.

"Berg has a way of playing at the very tail end of the beat," Odegard said. "You hear some drummers who are playing right on the beat, some who anticipate the beat, and they rush and they get into it in front. Bill Berg waits until there is nothing left, and then he hits the snare, in this case with his brush, and that just has a vacuum effect. It just sucks the listener in. They had this unmistakable freight train groove going. It was a brilliant take. We could do no wrong at that point. The vibe was so great that it was just fun for me. I was tapping my fingers listening to the thing. I couldn't believe where I was."

"Bill Berg taught me one of my biggest lessons," Inhofer said. "We were listening to the playback of 'Lily, Rosemary and the Jack of Hearts.' I'm sitting in the corner of the control room, and I'm watching Dylan and Bill Berg over by the speakers, and Bill's going, 'Okay, well I played it like this—ratata-tatta-tatta—but I could do it like this—ratatatatat.' I'm seeing a giant reservoir of talent, and it all comes down to a little spigot, and I'm seeing Bill Berg hand that spigot to Dylan, and he's saying, 'Here, turn on as much or as little as you want.' That lesson stuck with me through every session I've done in my whole life. I would rather have people say, 'That's a really great session, that's a really great commercial,' than say, 'Boy, that sucked, but listen to that keyboard player. Oooh.'"

Once again, as on the previous Friday night, Billy Peterson had to leave the session to go downtown and play bass with Natural Life—again with Dylan's blessing. But Dylan had one more song he wanted to try, and by the time he was ready to record a new version of the gentle ballad "If You See Her, Say Hello," reinforcements had arrived.

After sleeping for most of the afternoon, Peter Ostroushko was still feeling feverish from the pneumonia. But he was sick of being sick, so he dragged himself out of bed, crossed the street, and took up residence at the one spot that could reliably provide him some comfort and diversion: the pinball machine at the 400 Bar, kitty-corner from the New Riverside Cafe on Cedar and Riverside avenues.

"This is before cell phones," Ostroushko recalled in an interview in 2018. "So if people wanted to get a hold of you, they had to know where to call to find you, and back then everyone knew that if they called me at home and I wasn't there, the next best place for them to call would be at the 400 Bar, because I practically lived there when I wasn't at home." He was bumping away at the pinball machine in a fevered state when he heard owner Ted May growl at him from under his black

Jim Tordoff, Dave Hull, and Peter Ostroushko *(left to right)* in 1974. Photograph by Keith Hammerbeck.

walrus-style moustache: "Peter, there's a phone call for you." Ostroushko reluctantly abandoned the pinball game and walked to the far end of the bar where the phone was located. The call was from Jim Tordoff.

"I just got a phone call from Chris [Weber]," Tordoff said. "He says get our instruments and get down to Sound 80. I'll be by to pick you up in five minutes."

"Jim knew right away where to call," Ostroushko said. "And there is the serendipity in life, right there." Ostroushko left the 400 Bar, crossed the street, and went up to his apartment to get his fiddle and mandolin and excitedly await Tordoff's arrival.

Peter Ostroushko was born on August 12, 1953, into a Ukrainian immigrant family who lived in Minneapolis on Nicollet Island—a historic neighborhood less than a square mile in area, near the site of the first sawmill in Minneapolis, surrounded on all sides by the Mississippi River and connected to downtown by the Hennepin Avenue Bridge. "I had probably started playing my dad's mandolin when I was about three years old," Ostroushko said. "We were all pretty much immigrants, and I grew up with Ukrainian folk music. My dad played mandolin and guitar. All the adult figures in my life played something. Mandolin seemed to be the main instrument that most of them played, though. So we were always doing jam sessions, either at our house or somewhere else on Nicollet Island, where a lot of the Ukrainian immigrant community lived. Usually, they were just food fests and vodka fests. The music went on for hours and hours."

Whether it was inherited ability, endless practice, or a combination of both, Ostroushko was a prodigy with stringed instruments. When asked by interviewer David Edin in 2018 about his earliest influences, Ostroushko cited his father and friends, and "after that it was a cornucopia of mayhem": the Beatles, the Rolling Stones, Bill Monroe and the Bluegrass Boys, Neil Sedaka, Mozart, Eric Clapton, Frank Zappa and the Mothers of Invention, Roscoe Holcomb, J. S. Bach, Django Reinhardt, Lawrence Welk, Hank Williams, among others. Though mandolin was his first love, he picked up guitar and fiddle as well, and when he was a teenager in the 1960s, he gravitated toward rock music, as did so many of his generation.

"The first band I was in was all Ukrainian kids," Ostroushko recalled. "I played guitar and my older brother [George] was the lead singer. I don't remember what we called ourselves, but we used to rehearse at the Ukrainian American Home. We would play a strange hodgepodge of stuff. I remember playing a Sadie Hawkins dance at Edison High School, and we did all the hits of the time, 'Hey Joe' and 'Purple Haze' and 'Sunshine of Your Love.'"

"My older brother and I were kind of inseparable, and he was a bad influence on me," Ostroushko said. "I remember my tenth birthday. He gave me a big fat joint and said, 'Happy birthday. This is for you. I want you to smoke this all by yourself.' He was hanging out with some people from the West Bank at that time." The West Bank neighborhood had always attracted free spirits and exuded a bohemian flavor from its working-class roots. By the mid-'60s it was becoming a Twin Cities version of San Francisco's Haight-Ashbury, beckoning to musicians like Kevin Odegard and Chris Weber with its counterculture vibe.

Ostroushko's love for rock music continued unabated into the late 1960s. George began designing rock 'n' roll posters for Community News, the group that put on the Sunday night rock shows at the Labor Temple on Fourth Street and Central Avenue—gigs that featured the ultra-hip national bands of the late psychedelic/Woodstock era. A few like-minded local bands, such as Inhofer's Pepper Fog, sometimes were hired as opening acts.

"I was kind of on the periphery of that," Ostroushko said. "I was the younger brother, and they just let me hang out with them all the time. I think there were only two concerts that I didn't see, because it was just six blocks from my house. I grew up in that time period [February 1969 to November 1970]. Every Sunday there were these incredible rock acts that came through. The first one was the Grateful Dead. The second was a group from Chicago called Rotary Connection, and the front act was Jethro Tull. Nobody knew who they were—it was like their second gig in the United States. They played in New York City the night before, came to Minnesota, and then they were going to San Francisco after they left Minnesota. I remember actually sitting in the office when they got paid—five hundred dollars. And if you could imagine, five hundred dollars for a four-piece band traveling from England, that's like nothing. They played at the Fillmore West the next week, and their price shot up so high that they could never afford to bring them back."

Ostroushko's education with the counterculture included any number of brushes with musicians who were leading lifestyles far from the norms of the Ukrainian community. "I remember being in the backstage area for a Rod Stewart and the Faces concert, hanging out with these guys, and [guitarist] Ron Wood turning to me [motions getting a joint passed to him and taking a hit]: 'Here man!'"

It was a thrill for a young musician who lived for the edgy, San Francisco–style rock music of the era. But as the series of Labor Temple shows neared its end, his ears began to tell him it was time for a change. "One of the last concerts I remember seeing at the Labor Temple was the MC5," he said. "That was this wall of Marshall amplifiers, and I just could not stand the screaming guitars anymore. I mean, I really couldn't. That drove me into wanting to hear more acoustic music, which is where I came from to begin with, with my family."

By 1971, Ostroushko had gone back to concentrating on acoustic music and had hooked up with a group of folk and bluegrass musicians who played the West Bank clubs frequented by University of Minnesota students—the same neighborhood where eighteen-year-old college freshman Bobby Zimmerman from Hibbing had become Bob Dylan and traded his electric guitar for an acoustic Martin 00-17 after discovering folksingers Woody Guthrie and Odetta. Fresh out of high school, Ostroushko participated in his first jam session at the New Riverside Cafe, the first hippie-run vegetarian restaurant, performance space, and coffee hangout on the West Bank. Participants included folkies Dakota Dave Hull, Pop Wagner, and Robin Williams. The new kid asked if he could sit in, pulled out a fiddle from an unscarred case, and stunned the seasoned pickers with his skill, immediately establishing himself as the hot new player in town.

"I'm sure that's how I got to meet Becky Reimer," Ostroushko said. "She was one of the people who came to listen and would sit in.

I remember she was a fresh-faced, beautiful, clear-voiced singer who liked to sing country music. She asked me to play all these gigs with her, like free gigs at Powderhorn Park and ice cream socials. It didn't matter if we made five cents. I just liked making music."

"I started playing with Peter in '72," said Becky Reimer Thompson. "We did a four-piece—Peter, Jim Tordoff, Mike Cass on dobro, and me. Whoever booked the gig, it would be Becky Reimer and Friends, Mike Cass and Friends, Peter Ostroushko and Friends. Playing with him, I was always so amazed with his playing. Even back then he was just incredible and played with such emotion, and that just got more and more as he got older. I played with him for two years before I got up the nerve to ask him, 'Peter, do you like playing music with me?' He looked at me and he goes, 'Yeah.' And I said, 'Oh, okay.' He never said anything. He was very quiet. He would always give you this little smile of his, and you'd go, 'Oh, man, did I do something wrong?'"

"When I moved to the West Bank," Peter continued, "those were the people that I was hanging out with. Jim Tordoff and I would play at the Extemp, and at the New Riverside Café, and more and various and sundry permeations of bluegrass bands and stuff."

"Peter and I were in our first bluegrass band together," said Tordoff. "We would do busking in downtown Minneapolis together. We formed the nucleus for the house backup band at the Whole Coffeehouse at the University of Minnesota. They would bring in acts like John Hartford, Newgrass Revival, David Bromberg, and Norman Blake. For instance, when they had Vassar Clements come in, we basically were his band for the weekend he was here." Ostroushko eventually formed a partnership with Dakota Dave Hull.

One night after playing a gig with Tordoff at the Café Extempore, he walked into the nearby 400 Bar for a bump and a shot. "I meet this tall, lanky fellow with a beard and wire-rim glasses and a big floppy hat," Ostroushko said. "He introduces himself to me as Garrison Keillor. I knew exactly who he was because I'd been listening to his show on KSJN every morning from six to nine o'clock. My friends Bill Hinckley and Judy Larson did a lot of music with him. Garrison was playing the autoharp a little bit. They all sang. He informed me he had also started a radio show

Dakota Dave Hull and Peter Ostroushko onstage at Café Extempore in 1974. Photograph by Mike Shoo. Courtesy of Marge Ostroushko.

on Saturdays where live music would be done. He invited myself and Dakota Dave to come and be on his show. 'I'd love to. What does it pay?'"

"Don't worry, we'll pay you."

"We'll do it."

A month later, in the fall of 1974, Ostroushko and Hull were performing on *A Prairie Home Companion* at the Park Square Court in St. Paul. "Also, he asked Becky to be on the show quite frequently in the early days," Ostroushko said. "He liked singers, and with Becky, what was not to like? It seemed like from the first Saturday that we were on the show, we played almost every next Saturday till the end of the year. We were on the show all the time. I guess he liked our fast-filled music. That's all I could figure: it certainly wasn't the dulcet tone of our voices."

He and Hull began playing the college coffeehouse circuit, and when he had a few days free from touring, he played country-rock with Becky Reimer and the Sky Blue Water Boys. These were heady experiences for the young instrumentalist who was quickly developing his skills and local reputation, but he wasn't even a blip on the radar compared to an international superstar like Dylan. Yet when Dylan put in his request for a mandolin player, Ostroushko was Weber's first call.

Tordoff and Ostroushko wasted no time making the mile-and-a-half drive to Sound 80 from Ostroushko's West Bank apartment. "[Chris Weber] met us at the door and he led us into Studio A," Ostroushko recalled. "Bob Dylan was standing there in the shadows, and he came over. Chris introduced us."

Bob Dylan: instantly recognizable with his curly brown hair and unshaven face, the same face that had graced millions of album covers sold over the past dozen years. They shook hands, and the moment nearly overwhelmed Ostroushko. "God, I'm touching the hem of his garment," he recalled years later. "Here I am, standing in front of Bob Dylan. If I wasn't so sick, I think I would have fainted. I was trying to keep my mental faculties together."

Tordoff remembers that Dylan had been listening to the playback of "Lily, Rosemary and the Jack of Hearts" when they arrived.

"What have you got?" Dylan asked the two musicians, motioning to their cases.

"I have a banjo," Tordoff said.

"I don't hear a banjo on this. What do you have?" he asked Ostroushko.

"I have a fiddle and a mandolin."

"Oh, I think mandolin would sound really good on this one song," Dylan said.

Tordoff put his banjo back in its case. "And that was the end of my session with Bob Dylan," he said.

Ostroushko saw that the other musicians—Weber, Berg, Inhofer, and Odegard—were packing up their instruments. The studio lights had been turned down and the session appeared to be over. "But having the mandolin there made him want to record 'If You See Her, Say Hello' over," Ostroushko said.

"I think we're going to do one more," Dylan said to Weber. "Get your guitar."

"And so people started unpacking their instruments," Ostroushko said.

"I hung around for the rest of the evening," Tordoff said. "They

Becky Reimer and Peter Ostroushko in 1975. Courtesy of Marge Ostroushko.

didn't mind. I think probably they were sold on my qualifications as a hanger-on by Chris Weber. Of course, I was working with and for him. He said, 'These guys are okay. You don't need to worry about them.' I was pretty unobtrusive. I was in the control room with Paul Martinson. Of course, this was an adrenaline-fueled night, because there we were with Bob Dylan, after all."

By then, Becky Reimer had also arrived, but unlike Tordoff, she did not have an invitation. She had been at the Podium when Weber was gathering gear to go to the session, and when she found out that her friend Peter might get a chance to play with Bob Dylan, she decided to follow him into the studio. She was familiar with Sound 80, where she'd recorded a number of times.

"I went by myself," she said. "I snuck in, let me tell you." She continued:

I got in and I went to the restroom right way to hide out. I went in and I kind of snuck into the booth. Which was unbelievable that I got even that far. I was just watching everybody. I was so proud of Peter that I could hardly stand it. I wanted to go, "Go Peter!" I was just kind of hiding there, and the engineer—Paul Martinson—he looked at me and I went, "Sshhh . . . ." He just kind of smiled. And I stood in the corner and watched for a while. I got spotted by Dave Zimmerman, and I went, "Aw, shit." I was kind of panicked by the whole thing anyway, but I heard a little bit of it. I saw Bob, I saw Peter, and I was so amazed I could hardly talk. Bob's my hero, you know. I started singing songs when I was fourteen. When I first got my guitar, "Blowin' in the Wind" was one of the first songs I learned. I learned all his other songs. Every one of them.

She had met David Zimmerman but never did any sessions with him. The band had finished listening to "Lily, Rosemary and the Jack of Hearts" and was doing a run-through of "If You See Her, Say Hello" when Zimmerman spotted her in the control booth.

"Becky—" he said.

"How's it goin', David?" she replied.

"What are you doing here?"

"I just wanted to check it out."

"Well, let's go out now."

"I'd like to stay."

"You can't."

Reimer Thompson said Zimmerman was nice about it ("He didn't chase me out or anything") but insistent, so after being able to catch about twenty minutes of the session, she left the studio. "I never brought it up to anybody, because I felt kind of creepy about being in there because I wasn't supposed to be there," she said. "But I wore it like a badge of honor that I made it that far, because nobody was there. They were playing, then [Ostroushko] started playing, then I got kicked out."

The procedure for learning "If You See Her, Say Hello" followed the previous script. Dylan taught the song to Weber and disappeared while Weber taught it to the band. Tordoff was an interested observer of Dylan's process. "He is understated, but clearly his every nuance and wish would be closely followed," Tordoff said. "His brother stayed pretty much in the background until it was time to do the business agent stuff. Dylan was introverted like a poet. He had that sort of odd quality about him, but nobody thought much of it because that was his public persona. I would say his public persona and personal persona were well integrated. He was just the way then that he was always."

One of Ostroushko's most vivid memories of the evening was that Dylan was constantly smoking cigarettes between takes. "That's something that you'd never see anymore," Ostroushko said. "It's verboten to be smoking anywhere near equipment in a recording studio." Ostroushko was told that Dylan had just started smoking again after giving it up for several years. (He famously credited his smooth baritone on the albums *Nashville Skyline* and *Self Portrait* to the fact that he had quit smoking. "I tell you, you stop smoking those cigarettes, and you'll be able to sing like Caruso," he'd told *Rolling Stone* back in 1969.) Those days were behind him. His voice was back to its familiar pinched, nasal wail, but even in Ostroushko's fevered state, he noticed that Dylan's voice changed with every take of "If You See Her, Say Hello":

Dylan was smoking in between takes, and every time he would smoke a cigarette, his voice would change a little bit. So we would record something, and he would sit in the smoke and decide he didn't like what his voice sounded like, which seemed to be his criteria of what was going on. You know, it's his own personal performance. The band sounded great every time, but the cigarettes were having a real effect on his voice, and so in between each take he would decide, "Oh, I'm going to change the key." And he would, and then off he'd go: hit the record button.

And I am, like, let's see, what key are we in now? The record button's already on, and so I'm just, on the fly, trying to figure out what the chords are. In my mind I'm trying to think, "Okay, that was in C, so now we're in the key of E; no, now we're in D. Let's see, the relative minor of D is this." I'm just trying to do these changes in my mind. But he just starts strumming and singing. I think he started in C, and it progressively got higher until he eventually lands on—I believe it was—the key of D that we did that song in, where he thought that suited his voice best, and that's where it ended up being.

From Tordoff's perspective in the control room, the session was a smooth operation, thanks to Paul Martinson. "Paul was clearly the man there," Tordoff said. "He just mastered that. He was not intimidated [by Dylan] in the least. Totally, clearly there was respect going both ways between the two of them."

Dylan finally got a version of "If You See Her, Say Hello" that he liked. Ostroushko recalled listening to the final take in the control room, holding his mandolin, when Dylan asked him an odd question. "Can you make that [mandolin] sound like a flock of birds flying to the sky?" Attempting to figure out what Dylan meant, Ostroushko tried a few different styles and effects, including attempting a tremolo, but he couldn't come up with the sound Dylan was looking for.

"Can I play your mandolin?" Dylan asked him.

"Sure."

He handed the instrument to Dylan, who played a higher tremolo part and said, "I want that on the chorus." The song didn't actually have a chorus, but there was a vamp between verses that Dylan was playing.

"You mind if I go in and record that?" Dylan asked Ostroushko.

"Go ahead."

Dylan went back into the studio, where Martinson recorded him playing a tremolo part that was overdubbed on top of the original mandolin accompaniment that Ostroushko had laid down. The last notes of the Minneapolis sessions had been played. Dylan had the album he wanted.

"And then that was that," Ostroushko said. "That was the one tune that I played on, and after that it was all over."

One bit of business remained, however—paying the band. Inhofer remembers receiving a $400 check for Friday night, and another $400 check for Monday night, while Berg recalls the checks were for $300. Whatever the amount, they were straight union scale, sent from the Mark Zelenovich Advertising Agency, for whom David Zimmerman worked. The musicians were not asked to sign a release, and they were told they would not receive credit on the first run of albums, since the jackets had already been printed. "We were standing outside the control room, all the musicians and David Zimmerman," Inhofer said. "We were told that there were one hundred thousand copies pressed already that say Eric Weissberg & Deliverance, because that's who recorded all the tracks in New York under Phil Ramone's production. On the second pressing, if these hundred thousand sell out, your names will get on the second pressing. And we go, 'Okay, cool.'"

With that, everyone scattered: Bill Berg to California, Dylan back to his farm, Odegard back to the railroad, Peterson and Inhofer back to their fusion bands, and Ostroushko back to bed.

———————

Ostroushko woke up New Year's Eve morning with the grateful recognition that his fever had broken. The pneumonia he'd been suffering from for the past week was gone. As he lay in his bed, a smile came to his face. He recalled a wonderful, crazy fever dream he'd had during the night: that he and his banjo-playing pal Jim had been summoned to a local recording studio to lay down a track with Bob Dylan. It amused him how the mind can run wild when your body was fully engaged in trying to fight off an infection. What could be more absurdly preposterous than the idea of a twenty-one-year-old unknown Ukrainian folk musician from Northeast Minneapolis being asked to record with the great Bob Dylan—the Voice of His Generation, the composer of "Blowin' in the Wind" and "Mr. Tambourine Man," the most revered figure ever to emerge from the music clubs clustered around the University of Minnesota?

Crazy. So crazy that he had to share the details of the dream with Tordoff. He climbed down out of his bedroom loft and called the Podium. "Jim," Ostroushko said when Tordoff answered the phone. "I had the weirdest dream last night. You and I were on a recording session with Bob Dylan."

"That was no dream, buddy," Tordoff replied. He paused, letting the magnitude of the moment seep in, before gleefully telling Ostroushko, "You were there."

"What are you talking about?"

"We were at Sound 80 last night with Dylan. You played mandolin on a song that's going to be on his next album."

"No way."

"It's true."

For Ostroushko and the other Minneapolis musicians, their connection to *Blood on the Tracks* was a reality—and it was a connection that would continue to affect their lives for decades to come.

Billy Peterson had one final encounter with Dylan. He returned to Sound 80 on New Year's Day to collect some of his gear and encountered Dylan and his brother David in the icy parking lot, smoking cigarettes in David's car. They'd been in the studio attempting a final mix-down with Martinson, but as Martinson began cleaning up the sounds of the individual instruments, Dylan finally decided that he preferred the rough masters and would send those tracks to the pressing plant.

"I pulled my car up and I recognize David, but Bob was on the other side of David," Peterson said. "Dylan leaned over. I'm looking through the window, and I said, 'Bob, how ya doing, man?' He said, 'I want to really thank you for the music that you gave on these sessions. You bailed it all out. I really appreciate your playing, you and Bill. You guys did a great job. Thank you.' And that's the last I ever talked to him."

7

"They're Planting Stories in the Press"

THE EXHILARATION FELT IN MINNEAPOLIS BY THE SIX MUSICIANS who played on the *Blood on the Tracks* sessions was countered by despair in New York.

Phil Ramone's assistant engineer, Glenn Berger, described his and Ramone's reaction to the Minneapolis sessions in his autobiography: "When we returned from the Christmas holiday, Phil sat down with me, pale and dispirited. Bob had panicked. While visiting his family in Minnesota over the break, he had decided to re-record a bunch of the tracks in the nearby Twin Cities. Minneapolis was in its pre-Prince days; a recording nowhere-land. The only studio and musicians available were from the local jingle studio, where they recorded commercials for Mom's Biscuits and the Oldsmobile dealership on Nicollet Avenue." Berger's response to Dylan's course change was reflective of the dismissive attitude many music industry insiders had for any work done outside of New York or Los Angeles. They'd never been to Sound 80, or worked with Paul Martinson, or heard of the six musicians who re-recorded half the album. How could it be any good?

"Phil handed me the new master tapes," Berger wrote.

> It was my job to cut out the tracks we had worked on, and splice in the new ones he had done in bum-fuck Minnesota. My breathing stopped as I listened to the stuff that was going to replace what we had done. . . . These searing, wrenching, burning, bloody songs . . .

turned into bouncy little jingles? What? I cut into the tape like an old, drunken, western surgeon with a rusty knife. I cut out pink, vibrating, living, breathing body parts and left them bleeding on the floor. It wasn't my job to choose, it was my job to plunge in the blade and kill the baby that I had helped deliver. The album came out a few weeks later. When I got a copy, I quickly flipped it to the back. That's where the unsung heroes of recording look first. We take it all for the glory, but we also like the credit. I looked at every word of the smallest type but was to find myself suffering the final indignity. No credit. My name nowhere on the cover.

He wasn't the only one.

Blood on the Tracks was released by Columbia records on January 20, 1975—scarcely three weeks after the final recording session at Sound 80. As David Zimmerman had told the Minneapolis Six, their names were nowhere to be found on the album jacket. Instead, the brief credits listed Tony Brown on bass, Buddy Cage on steel guitar, Paul Griffin on organ, and Eric Weissberg and Deliverance. As a band, Weissberg and Deliverance appear on only one song, "Meet Me in the Morning," which also includes Buddy Cage's sole appearance, an overdubbed pedal steel part. Tony Brown underpins Dylan's acoustic guitar on four of the five tracks from the New York session. Griffin—the towering talent who played on Dylan's breakthrough rock albums in the mid-'60s, as well as on "American Pie," "In the Midnight Hour" and "Brown-Eyed Girl"—does not play on any of the ten songs. Half of the album came directly from the two sessions at Sound 80, though the record-buying public would not know that unless they paid close attention to the album's reviews.

Those reviews were overwhelmingly positive. Paul Williams of the *Soho News* wrote: "I have already played this record more times in the past week than I play most records in a year. I love it. It is one of Dylan's best albums. It is probably the best album of the last five years."

Peter Knobler of *Crawdaddy* wrote that *Blood on the Tracks* "is an extraordinary album. The question isn't whether it is Dylan's best album since *Blonde on Blonde*, but whether it is *the* best album since *Blonde on Blonde*."

Greil Marcus, Dylan's most withering critic during his *Self Portrait* period, wrote in *Rolling Stone*: "Just as casual listening fills one with delight at Dylan's testing of his genius, a close listening can be shattering, terrifying. It goes without saying that no one else in rock & roll could make a record like this."

Ellen Willis of the *New Yorker* wrote: "On this record the relationship between Dylan's self and his persona seems richer, scarier and more intense than it has in years."

Michael Gray, author of an exhaustive study of Dylan's career called *Song and Dance Man*, called it "the most strikingly intelligent album of the seventies."

Of course, not everyone was bowled over by the record. Dave Marsh wrote in *Rolling Stone*: "Though the music and lyrics may echo his greatest work, that's all they do. The long songs, particularly, suffer from flat, tangled imagery, and the music, with all its hints at the old glory, is often incompetently performed. I suppose it's all a matter of what you're willing to settle for."

The brilliant, cranky Lester Bangs described the album in *Creem* as "at worst an instrument of self-abuse, at best innocuous as a crying towel and certainly was not going to make me a better person or teach me anything about women, myself or anything else but how painfully confused Bob Dylan seemed to be."

The album had been out for almost two months by the time Jon Landau—originally a rock critic, but now shifting gears to become the producer of Bruce Springsteen's brilliant *Born to Run* album, weighed in. From his opinion piece in the March 13, 1975, issue of *Rolling Stone*:

> The record itself has been made with typical shoddiness. The accompanying musicians have never sounded more indifferent. The sound is generally no more than what Greil Marcus calls "functional," a neutral environment from which Dylan emerges.... If in Dylan's world of extremes there's room for a middle ground, that's where I place *Blood on the Tracks*. It's his best album since *Blonde on Blonde*, but not nearly as good. If it contains nothing so bad as the second version of "Forever Young," only "Tangled Up in Blue"

comes even close to "One of Us Must Know (Sooner or Later)." To compare the new album to *Blonde on Blonde* at all is to imply that people will treasure it as deeply and for as long. They won't.

The consensus from those who praised the album seemed to suggest that Dylan had succeeded despite rather than because of his sidemen. There was Robert Christgau's positive review in the *Village Voice*, which called *Blood on the Tracks* Dylan's most mature album, "utilizing unknown Minneapolis studio musicians who impose nothing beyond a certain anonymous brightness on the proceedings."

Paul Nelson, expressing yet another view of the album in *Rolling Stone*, said: "Dylan's subtlety, intelligence, depth of feeling and overall artistry have created a flexible and complex ambiguousness which somehow fuses an elegiac tone with the most muscular, confident style. . . . Even the near anonymous, ordinary Minneapolis musicians do better than the more gifted but overrated Band."

If the critics were mostly aware that the credits on the album were incomplete, the public didn't care. Sales were extraordinary, even for Dylan. It shot to number one on the Billboard chart, and by February 12—three weeks after its release—the album had sold five hundred thousand copies. That far exceeded the first run of one hundred thousand that David Zimmerman had promised would trigger a reprint of the jacket with proper credits. That never happened. To date, *Blood on the Tracks* is Dylan's best-selling studio album (excluding his first two greatest hits volumes), having sold two and a half million copies worldwide. And yet the credits—to Brown, Cage, Griffin, and Weissberg and Deliverance—have never been changed in all subsequent issues of the album.

———————

Bill Berg bought his copy of *Blood on the Tracks* in Venice, California. He'd gone almost directly from the Sound 80 Studio to his white Volvo and trailer and then to the West Coast. Upon hearing the album, he thought the music was worthy of comparison to some of his other Dylan favorites, including "Like a Rolling Stone" and "Lay Lady Lay." "I don't think I've ever heard Bob more emotional," Berg said. "I'm not a total fanatic—I don't know every song on every album—but 'If You See Her, Say Hello' brings tears to your eyes. That's how good that stuff was. He was coming from a deep place in his psyche to do that."

Berg hoped to find steady work in the star-studded California music industry. He found opportunities to play with some outstanding musicians, but his résumé didn't overly impress anyone. "I thought *Blood on the Tracks* might open doors, but in the LA music scene at the time, it was, 'Okay, Bob has a new record out, you're the drummer . . . ,'" Berg said. "I didn't get much traction at the time."

Berg was sanguine about the omission, however. "They're not going to redo the printing of tens of thousands of jackets," he said. As he recalled:

> There's a number of reasons why they didn't. Bob wasn't pushing for it, and nobody else was. I recall the days before *Blood on the Tracks*, on some of the famous jazz albums there never was the whole band mentioned, just the leader. Just the artists and the names of the songs. They had to mention the songwriter, and BMI or ASCAP. We were just coming to an era when musicians were being mentioned. We were in the crosshairs of that. That's why the Wrecking Crew documentary came out. All those [uncredited] guys were part of every one of the Beach Boys sessions—Howard Roberts, Hal Blaine, Tommy Tedesco, Glen Campbell.
>
> For me it [the Dylan session] was one of these anomalies, something strange that happens once. Frankly, I wanted to be known as a session or fusion drummer more than a folk drummer. But that being said, I like to be a chameleon that can do a lot of different kinds of things. Right after *Blood on the Tracks* was released, *Rolling Stone* had a big article about the Minneapolis musicians. For me, if there was a wound from not being included, that helped. This keeps following us. We have gotten royalty checks for *Blood on the Tracks* ever since. I still get one check a year for the latest re-release or box set or whatever. It can run from a very thin year, from $35 or $40, to $500 or $600 or a little more. The others get it, too.

When Berg was still doing session work in the Twin Cities, he met jazz guitarist Howard Roberts, who had come to town for a guitar clinic. "He said, 'If you come to LA, let's talk,'" Berg said. "It's always nice when you're jumping to another city to have some gigs to start with. I never recorded with Howard Roberts. There were live recordings, but no official releases with me on drums."

His next significant musical collaboration was with Michael Pinder, the original keyboard player for the Moody Blues. Berg was the drummer on Pinder's 1976 solo album, *The Promise.* Berg invited Jimmy "Flim" Johnson, bassist for the Minnesota jazz-rock band Flim and the BB's, to join him in California for the recording sessions. "That was an album with no tour possibilities," Berg said. "[Pinder had] left the Moody Blues earlier, but he still wanted to write and record. He was quite British. Every single morning, he would have his English breakfast tea. It took a number of days. We recorded in Malibu on a beautiful ranch called Indigo Ranch. I think it did pretty well, but it didn't attain any gold status. I actually listened to it a few months ago, on YouTube. It sounds a little dated, especially my drum fills, but I think the record holds together. It has a lot of heart."

Berg moved to Monterey for a while and identified himself as a session drummer at a little area studio that attracted some big-name clients. He picked up some work and made a few notable contacts. "I bumped into Cat Stevens, who was trying to produce an album for his guitar player, Alun Davies," Berg said. "Jon Mark of the Mark-Almond Band was also instrumental in putting those sessions together. I loved Cat Stevens's music, of course. [The Davies album] never was released—it fizzled out."

Berg moved back to Minnesota in 1977, "just to pick up the slack of not getting the proper amount of work on the West Coast, because I was brand new. Any studio town—New York, Nashville, LA—you have to wait to move up the ladder. I was playing locally, but it was hand to mouth." He returned to Sound 80, reunited with Billy Peterson and Natural Life, and played on albums by singer-songwriters Mark Gaddis, Dick Pinney, and Gamble Rogers in addition to another Leo Kottke record and picking up a full schedule of jingle work.

Then, in 1977, Cat Stevens called. "He asked did I want to record in Europe for him," Berg said. "I said, 'Let's do this.' I don't think he knew or cared about *Blood on the Tracks*. He and I really didn't talk about it." Stevens was nearing the end of his run of Top 40 hits and chart-topping albums. He was also about to convert to Islam and change his name to Yusuf Islam, a step that would essentially take him out of the pop music field for the next three decades. "We went over to a studio in Amsterdam and didn't get one track out of those sessions," Berg said. "Not one track did he like. Cat was so disappointed with the European results, he asked me, 'Do you know anywhere in the States where we could keep this going?' I said, 'I worked at Sound 80 for years. That's where I would recommend.' I think Cat Stevens was the producer, and Tom Jung was the engineer. There were no other local musicians, just me, because he brought his whole band over to play at Sound 80. Everybody was there for at least a couple of weeks."

The album Stevens was working on, *Izitso*, would be his penultimate pop album until 2006's *An Other Cup*. As with many of the most popular pop artists of the late '70s, Stevens's process of making *Izitso* was an exercise in bloated self-indulgence—a wild divergence from Bob Dylan's style of stripped-down, rapid-fire production. "Bob was very unassuming, but there were occasions we had people like Cat Stevens come in, and they took over the studio," Herb Pilhofer said. "They literally had incense all over the place, and cases of nuts. It became their own environment."

"All the super groups of those days, Fleetwood Mac, etc., would take weeks and weeks because the budgets were so large," Berg said. "The big artists didn't necessarily want to fly to Minneapolis, even with the good reputation Sound 80 had in those days. It's out of the way. Cat Stevens was bored to death. He would ask, 'Are there any restaurants in Minneapolis?'"

In 1978, Berg recorded on a Flim and the BB's album, engineered by Paul Martinson and produced by Tom Jung at Sound 80. It was one of the first two digital recordings done at the studio. Yet aside from that groundbreaking project and Cat Stevens's *Izitso*, Berg's return to Minneapolis became "pretty much weddings, bar mitzvahs—supermarket openings, as we used to call them," Berg said. Another relocation—and a career change—seemed necessary. Berg, his first wife and their son Jacob moved back to California in 1979. This time, Berg was determined to resume his work in the art world. "I thought, here's my chance to do this animation thing," he said. "I put a portfolio in to CalArts, the school Walt Disney always dreamed of—a multidiscipline school. [They taught] both character animation and fine arts animation—uncommercial—and an acting branch, a music branch, and a fine arts oil painting/abstract branch. It was by far more comprehensive than the Chicago school."

The school was funded by the Disney corporation; Berg was able to afford the tuition with money left over from his GI Bill and received a scholarship the second year. "We had classes every day, many drawing and design classes that would round you out as an artist," he said. "There are different aspects of making animated film. The layout department did backgrounds—the places for characters to perform: Swiss Alps, California desert, Italian village. There were layout classes, animation classes, and several other disciplines."

At the end of the school year, students at CalArts were required to make a short film between thirty seconds and three minutes. "Then they had a show of all the student work, and who shows up but some of the great Disney animators—Walt called them the Nine Old Men—to look at your cute, funky, stupid films," Berg said. "Mine was called *The Jam*. This little Black sax player was going to sit in at a club. Nobody thought he could play, and he blew them all away. The voice of the main character was done by Billy Peterson. His cousin Tommy Peterson was the sax player." (Tommy played in *NBC's Tonight Show* band with Doc Severinsen for more than a decade.)

Berg was hoping to be hired as a Disney animator, but his film and portfolio didn't win over the judges, and he was turned down. He took a job at a company called Filmation, which did Saturday morning cartoons such as *Fat Albert*, among others. "They had a Lone Ranger thing, sort of a sci-fi half-hour," Berg said. "Just typical Saturday morning stuff, but I had a job in the animation industry, and that was cool. I did that for a summer—one season. The way the animation industry works was it was very seasonal. You work from spring right on through the summer, and you had to do one show a week. The show would come on a week later. It was a breakneck pace."

Even so, Berg found time while at Filmation to work on another portfolio of drawings of animals and anything else he could think of to catch the eye of the Disney animation department. In 1982, Berg's portfolio was accepted and he was hired as an animator by Disney, where he met his second wife, Kaaren Lundeen, a Swedish professional oil painter. "We both put our portfolios in within a week of each other," Berg said. They started a Disney animation training program together in February 1982. "Disney was everyone's goal," he said. "They had that great track record from the '30s through the '70s. In the early '80s, Walt had passed away, a lot of his major animators and designers were getting up in years, and animation was being taken care of by Ron Miller, his son-in-law. Ron's attitude was, 'Do we still have to make these animated movies?'" Even Berg had cause to wonder why the studio was bothering with their current animation projects. "Our first project was a short subject that wasn't very good, called *Mickey's Christmas Carol*," Berg said. "One of the animators on that was a guy named John Lasseter. He turned out to be one of the principal creative minds, along with Steve Jobs, that put Pixar together. I knew him a little bit and knew he was destined for bigger things."

Berg's other initial project was another middling feature called *The Black Cauldron*. It came at a time when Disney animation was "still reeling," in Berg's words. The company was nearly taken over by the Bass brothers, two rich Texans who intended to buy up Walt Disney Productions and split the theme parks, filmmaking division, and consumer division into different companies. "Roy Disney, Walt's nephew, came in with some of the most powerful Hollywood people—Jeffrey Katzenberg, Michael Eisner, and Peter Schneider, who ran animation," Berg said. "They started to look within the company to find the most talented people to make the next movie and took us away from the very mediocre *Black Cauldron*."

Berg says the picture that turned the company around was *The Great Mouse Detective*, a Sherlock Holmes takeoff featuring the voice of

Vincent Price. That was followed by *Oliver and Company* and *The Rescuers Down Under,* a stretch of artistically and commercially successful films that set up Disney's spectacular renaissance in the '90s. "That was the beginning of 'Let's do animated musical pictures again,'" Berg said. "And there comes *The Little Mermaid, Beauty and the Beast, Aladdin,* and *The Lion King*—there's your big four. We contributed to all of them."

Along with his wife, Kaaren, Berg supervised dozens of animators on *Little Mermaid.* "We headed up the Ariel department," Berg said. "I did the Beast with dozens and dozens of other artists, and Kaaren worked on Belle, then after that we both worked on the Aladdin character, and we both worked on Simba—the adult version—from *Lion King.* I'll liken this to a band like The Police. In The Police's heyday, everybody wanted to hear the next record, and we felt people couldn't wait for our next feature, because we were on a roll. I would say I reached a peak. I wanted to be hands-on with the drawing aspect, as opposed to just coordinating as department head. I liked the fact that I was still drawing every day."

And playing drums at night. "As busy as I got at Disney, I still wanted to play live in clubs in LA at that time," he said. He was cofounder of the Wayne Johnson Trio with the Grammy Award–winning guitarist. They were joined by fellow Minneapolis transplant Jimmy Johnson on bass and played once or twice a month in some of the best venues in Los Angeles, including the Baked Potato, which is still operating. "Living in LA, you had all these great studio bands—Tom Scott's band [L.A. Express] that backed Joni Mitchell formed at the Baked Potato. You weren't playing a lot because there were so many great bands. We'd go up the coast and down to San Diego. I was a busy guy. This band rehearsed once a week, which is why we got so good."

Berg and Johnson recorded a handful of albums with the Wayne Johnson Trio, including *Arrowhead* (1980), *Everybody's Painting Pictures* (1982), *Grasshopper* (1983), *Spirit of the Dancer* (1988), and *Keeping the Dream Alive* (1993.) Berg also reunited with Leo Kottke in Los Angeles, where he drummed on the 1994 album *Peculiaroso,* produced by singer-songwriter Rickie Lee Jones. "She was a little difficult to work with, not to be disparaging," Berg said. "But the project still turned out good. John Leftwich, a bass player who played in the Wayne Johnson Trio, was bass player for Rickie Lee."

Berg and Kaaren worked at Disney for twenty-one years, from 1982 to 2003. They knew it was time to leave when Disney reached an even greater level of success with computer animation. "It was pretty obvious to us after we finished *Lion King* that the computer revolution was taking over," he said. "Right about that time, they released *Toy Story*. The thought was that could make $25 to $30 million in total. It made $25 million the very first weekend. I still love the hand-animated drawing. I still love those cel animations. The computer-generated ones were a little stiff and robotic, and as far as I'm concerned, it always comes down to story first."

Billy Peterson heard *Blood on the Tracks* as soon as it was released and loved it. "I went 'Wow, that turned out great,'" he said.

> Quite frankly, it was just one of many sessions I did in those days. I didn't know if it was going to live. Then I saw it in print, and they got the wrong names on the record. Tony [Brown] did all the shit in New York, and I did the shit here, but they didn't get our frickin' names right. So anyway, I blew it off. It didn't affect me one way or another. Just another thing that happened. I didn't really care about getting the proper credits. To me it was just another fuckup in the industry. But the credibility was huge, playing on a hit with Dylan. You never plan on this. All of a sudden I'm sitting on a number-one hit with the biggest artist in the world, and I didn't even think it was going to make it onto the record. It wells up underneath you like a fucking tsunami. It becomes this big deal. I had no plans of any of these things ever happening in my life, to record with a major pop star like that.

Despite the credibility and the unforgettable experience, he didn't see any direct benefit from playing on the album. He believes the issue of who played on which track was too "underground" for most casual listeners, though the industry certainly knew. "You could tell immediately what was recorded in New York and what was in Minneapolis," he said.

> No doubt about it. We really didn't care what those guys did in New York. We didn't hear the New York stuff. We just threw on what we threw on. All the cats, we weren't trying to cop it. I think Dylan was looking for different input from the musicians. That's why he was so open on those sessions. He dug what he heard. Because we did two days, just this whirlwind of two days, that just happened. Making the Grammy Hall of Fame? Shit, who would have planned on that? Those things only happen to musicians if their nose is in the wind the right way. You fall into different places. Sometimes you're in the right place at the right time. Ben Sidran says you throw it out, let history decide how great it is, what you've done. History decided. It's about the journey. Some of the greatest things will go unnoticed, and some of things you never plan on will be successful.

If Peterson was aware of the disappointment in some circles that greeted the re-recording of half the album's songs, he didn't let it bother him. "I didn't give a shit what anybody thought," he said. "It was just another two days of my life. I'm not making light of it, because I really enjoyed being on a platinum record, but that kind of success is like a time lock on a safe. You beat your head against it, and when the time is right, the safe opens up and you fall through the door. That's exactly what happened to all of us."

After *Blood on the Tracks*, Billy Peterson continued to play with Natural Life as well as maintain his busy schedule as a session bassist, playing on countless jingles as well as contributing bass on albums by Leo Kottke (*Chewing Pine*), Steve Young, Mark Gaddis, and Gamble Rogers. "I worked long hours in the studio, five and six days a week, all through the early '70s and even into 1980 at Sound 80," Peterson said. "Herb [Pilhofer] was doing commercials, movie scores, soundtracks all through the '80s. I was doing no major tours, because I had young kids." Like

Dylan in the late 1960s, Peterson's family obligations kept him mostly homebound. Despite his growing reputation as a bass virtuoso, he never seriously thought about relocating. "I was so busy here, making so much money, my plate was so full," he said. "There was plenty of work to do here. The music scene was so vibrant here. I never aspired to do that."

With one exception. In 1977, Peterson heard that jazz piano great Bill Evans was auditioning bass players to replace the departing Eddie Gomez. Peterson moved to New York for the summer and auditioned for Evans at the Village Vanguard. "I was talking to Helen Keane [Evans's manager and producer]," Peterson said. "She knew about my bass playing. My wife let me go there and hang out all summer. I was hanging at the Village Vanguard. Bill was there; I knew him to say hi, and he knew about my playing, but he was going to take Marc Johnson on a tour. He took him to Copenhagen and kept him. Johnson was a magnificent bass player, and the drummer, Smokin' Joe LaBarbera, was also a good friend of mine. I wanted to play with Bill so bad. He was a great mentor of mine. I grew up listening to him. Scott LaFaro—that's the way I approach bass. [LaFaro was the original bassist in the Evans trio; he died in a car accident in 1961.] Scott was the guy who broke the mold." Peterson added: "When I smelled an opportunity, I never closed the door. I learned a lesson from a guy who had a chance to join Ahmad Jamal and blew it off. But I never got the gig, so I went back to Minneapolis to the Longhorn gig."

Natural Life recorded three albums in the late '70s—*Natural Life*, *Unnamed Land*, and *All Music*. Bill Berg played drums on two of the albums and designed the covers for all three. Natural Life held their two-to-three nights per week residency at the Longhorn in downtown Minneapolis through 1978. "We spent a lot of time trying to get signed nationally, and our records hold up pretty good," Peterson said. "We were making good money—then the punk scene was coming in. They were downstairs and we were upstairs." The punks eventually drove fusion out of the building.

"We split up, doing different things," Peterson said. "[Bob] Rockwell leaving—that instigated the breakup with the band." Saxophonist Rockwell moved to New York to play with Tito Puente, Berg returned to

California, and his replacement, Eric Gravatt, rejoined McCoy Tyner's band.

During the late '70s, Peterson rekindled his love for a quintessentially northern sport: speedskating. His first keyboard teacher, Ernie Garvin—who'd played with Peterson's parents in the WCCO radio orchestra—was also a speedskating fan who encouraged Peterson to compete in the sport. "I had been a junior champion speedskater," Peterson said. "Ernie Garvin got me into speedskating because he had five kids who were national champions. He got me going to the time trials for the Olympics until I was thirty or thirty-one—until 1980. I started winning national medals in 1977–78."

When he was twenty-six, Peterson was nationally ranked as a speedskater. He and his wife started traveling to West Allis, Wisconsin, home to one of only two indoor speedskating rinks in America, where he skated in time trials, along with another skating hotshot named Eric Heiden. "I was out of shape, so I started skating again and, through the back door, got really good. My wife said, 'You've got five minutes left to do this,' and gave me the nod. I went to Milwaukee on weekends, came back during the week, and trained in Minneapolis. That's what I did through the later '70s. I didn't make the Olympic team, but Eric Heiden did," Peterson said. Heiden won five gold medals at the 1980 Winter Olympic games in Lake Placid, New York. "I didn't completely quit skating until I was about forty-nine years old."

About the time that Natural Life was breaking up, Peterson met jazz singer-songwriter Ben Sidran. "We were at Sound 80 when David Rivkin contacted me," Peterson said. "I knew David way back in the '70s. He was in the studio with Prince, doing demos for 'Little Red Corvette.' He knew Sidran was looking for a guy who could play upright bass and electric styles. He got me an audition in '78. I started touring with Ben, and I've played with him for the past forty-three years. I'm still playing with Ben Sidran." They made many records together, beginning with *Lover Man*, recorded at Minneapolis's Cookhouse studio in 1984, and continuing with *On the Cool Side* (1985), *Spread Your Wings and Fly Now!!* (1988), *Too Hot to Touch* (1988), *Cool Paradise* (1990), *Live in Japan* (1992, with brother Ricky Peterson on synthesizer), *Nick's Bump* (2003),

A Salute to Ben Webster (2003, with Bob Rockwell), *Live à Fip* (2005, with Rockwell), and *Blue Camus* (2014).

Along the way, Sidran introduced Peterson to future Rock & Roll Hall of Famer Steve Miller. Sidran and Miller had met in 1961 at the University of Wisconsin in Madison, where they formed a band called the Ardells with Boz Skaggs. Sidran was not an original member of the Steve Miller Band but played keyboard on several of the band's albums in the late '60s and early '70s. In 1988, Miller hired Sidran to produce his side project, the jazz-oriented *Born 2B Blue*. Sidran in turn hired the Peterson brothers, Billy and Ricky, to play on that album with Miller. "Steve loved the band so much, he hired the whole band to go on the road with him," Peterson said. "I was in the band from 1987 to 2010."

So were his brothers Paul Peterson on guitar (1988, 1991–92) and Ricky Peterson on keyboards (1988, 1991). Billy Peterson recorded two studio albums with the Steve Miller Band, playing bass and piano on the albums *Wide River* (1993) and *Let Your Hair Down* (2010) in addition to steady touring. "Most of the time it was huge venues, amphitheaters, mostly in the summer," Peterson said. "Not as many indoor gigs. Session work didn't take up all my time. During those years, I kept doing a lot of jazz stuff."

When he wasn't on the road or recording with Sidran and Miller, Peterson was busy recording and producing albums for himself and others. Beginning in 1984, he produced and played bass for his sister Linda Peterson's *Too Late to Leave Early* and his mother Jeanne Peterson's *Triplicity*, and then extended the favor to his sister Patty on *The More I See You* (1989) and brother Ricky on *Smile Blue* (1991, recorded at Prince's Paisley Park). He produced Minnesota folk singer Larry Long's albums *Sweet Thunder* (1987) and *Well May the World Go* (2000). In 1998, he began producing a series of After Hours jazz CDs featuring soloists Bob Rockwell, Bill Carrothers, Bob Malach, David Hazeltine, and Lee Konitz.

———————

Sound 80 proved conclusively with the Dylan session that it could match the quality of any studio in the country. In fact, the studio continued to push the boundaries of audio engineering when the

3M Company in St. Paul developed a prototype digital recording system. "What now is done by Sony and Mitsubishi and all of the biggies was started in the '70s by 3M," Herb Pilhofer said. "We became their kitchen in the backyard. We had the opportunity to work with some of the earliest digital recordings. I myself produced an album with the first thirty-two-track digital recording that was ever developed. Sound 80 developed an amazing reputation nationally in terms of being the first all-digital studio. There were a number of other things that, in my mind, were equally important in terms of development."

When Glenn Berger snidely referred to Sound 80 as a jingle house, he was technically accurate. But then, his own A&R Studios did plenty of jingles and trailed Sound 80 when it came to technical innovation. "A jingle house?" Bill Berg said. "We did a lot of jingles, but we also did some really, at that time, state-of-the-art recordings. I did two projects with Natural Life and Flim and the BB's, their very first project, called Direct-to-Disc. You set the instruments and mics up, but instead of going to tape, then mix down, it's a live performance cut direct-to-disc. It took a studio like Sound 80, which was much more than a jingle house—and we can thank Tom Jung for this. It was slightly before digital. Sound 80 was one of the first studios to do that. There was a record company called Sheffield Labs that did direct-to-disc, too. That means between songs they don't stop the cutter head from making the impression on the disc. You have to stop playing, be very quiet, and do the count-off silently for the next song. It really was nerve-wracking. If you make a mistake—you're twenty minutes into the first side, and you make big train wreck at 18:35—they have to throw the disc out. It's done. There's a lot of pressure, but to Tom Jung's credit, he'd say, 'We're here to make a final product, and if we throw a few discs away, we're good.'"

Along with Flim and the BB's, the first group to be digitally recorded by Sound 80 was the Saint Paul Chamber Orchestra. The SPCO album won the Grammy Award for best chamber orchestra recording in 1979. Unfortunately, innovation and reputation alone could not guarantee that Sound 80 would flourish indefinitely. In fact, six years after Dylan recorded there, the studio closed. "In 1981, I decided to dissolve the company," Pilhofer said. "There were so many things on the horizon. You could see the advent of cheap synthesizers and equipment. For $10,000 you could put up a little basement studio and put out stuff: if you were anywhere musically inclined, that was acceptable. It was pretty good—but a lot of people don't know the difference between pretty good and very good. By '81, it was time to stop it. We had a great run."

Tom Jung started his own company and left for New York. Paul Martinson died in 2012. The building was sold and eventually became the headquarters of Orfield Laboratories, an independent multisensory design research lab that converted the original Studio A into what the *Guinness Book of World Records* has listed as "the quietest place on earth."

"There was a point when I was getting frustrated," Pilhofer said. "I was no longer the photographer working in the dark room—I was being the photographer running the business with twenty-five people. I had to stop that. I went back to making music. That was unavoidable in a way. Look, Bob Dylan gave it a lot of recognition, and getting a Grammy Award was a lot of recognition, but it didn't really pay the phone bills. It was the fact that Sound 80 could also record school bands, choirs, all kinds of average stuff. We also developed a label and turned out very excellent quality twelve-inch LPs. We had a multitude of activities that in many ways paid for something you really wanted to do. At times it was not very easy, but we always kept it going, and we had a great time at it. It was a wonderful experience."

8

"All You Can Do Is Do What You Must"

AS WITH BERG AND PETERSON, THE RELEASE OF *BLOOD ON THE*
Tracks didn't create any other musical opportunities for Gregg Inhofer.
In fact, he was snubbed by Dylan in person a few months after *Blood on the Tracks* was released. Inhofer was at a Minneapolis club to see Brian Setzer and the Stray Cats. He found himself standing in the back of the room near Dylan, who was checking out the band as a possible opening act for a future tour. "I walked over and said, 'Hi, Bob. Gregg Inhofer. I played on the *Blood on the Tracks* session.' He turned and said, 'Oh, yeah.' Then he turned away. We didn't bond."

Inhofer had not been waiting anxiously for his big moment on Dylan's new album to hit the stores. Nor did he pursue a performing credit after the album turned out to be a huge hit. Rather than expanding the credits, the second pressing of the album jacket removed them all. "My conspiracy theory on why we never got credited: we did not sign W-2s, we did not sign releases," Inhofer said. "The legal department at Columbia went nuts. 'What do you mean they didn't sign any releases?' I could have sued them. I added a chord on 'You're a Big Girl Now.' I could have said I cowrote the damn song. I didn't sign any release. I think they were worried. So I think what they did was say, 'Okay, listen, it's not like we're working with New York cats. These are Minnesota kids. Let's just see what happens if we take everybody's name off. See if anybody complains.' Nobody did."

Now Inhofer kicks himself for not objecting when David Zimmerman's promise of credits was broken:

> I was young and naive. I don't think I've ever been pissed off. I felt pragmatically we were wronged. What they did was wrong. John Farrar, who worked with Olivia, told us when you have a hit, money seems to come from everywhere, because everybody wants to re-create the magic, everybody wants to use the same studio, the same instruments, the same musicians, the same producer, the same engineer, what kind of drugs were they doing (was it Peruvian or Colombian cocaine?), what kind of booze—they want to re-create the magic, and we never got a chance to do that. But that didn't happen, you know, because we didn't get our names on there. Had our names been on there, with the notoriety of the album, there's a good shot that maybe some new artist coming up would go, "Yeah, I need a band to go on tour. Hey, let's get those guys from *Blood on the Tracks* from the Minneapolis sessions." It could have happened. But am I bitter about it? No.

Inhofer also said he is not bitter that This Oneness quit backing Olivia Newton-John due to an ultimatum from their drummer. "Bernie Pershey said, 'Either we quit Olivia in two weeks or I'm leaving the band.' So we quit Olivia in two weeks, and a month later he left the band. What the hell?"

Newton-John first asked Dale Strength to stay on as her music director, but he declined. Then she asked if he and Inhofer would stay as codirectors. "We turned her down," Inhofer said. "Had we gone, I'd probably be dead . . . free-base was really big at the time. I'd be dead. I'm a recovering alcoholic. All roads lead to now."

The time had come for This Oneness to make their own try for the big time. In 1975, they released an album called *Surprize*, recorded at Cookhouse Studio in Minneapolis. It was classic mid-'70s progressive rock, with songs that ran together as suites featuring random noises, shouts, and rapid instrumental soloing. There was even a cut called "Song for Olivia." Released on the Oz label, the album didn't sell much.

This Oneness recorded two more albums that weren't released, and by 1977 the band changed its name, size, and focus. Now called Brainiac, the band was a three-piece consisting of Inhofer, Strength, and the rein-stated Pershey. Instead of doing prog-fusion originals in an attempt to create a singular identity, Brainiac did popular rock cover songs for the bar crowd. "We were doing all rock, like Kiss, Foreigner, Styx, Journey, all that stuff," Inhofer said. "I was playing keybass, Bernie had his Au-tostick. We were doing the five-state area, Chicago, Milwaukee, Madison, Tyndall, South Dakota. We were booked fifty-three out of sixty-five days. We're out there singing Journey, and people come up to us and say, 'Hey, can you do "Don't Stop Believin'"?' And we'd say, 'Listen, even Steve Perry doesn't sing Steve Perry six nights in a row.' Give me a break."

Like many musicians around the country, Brainiac had a one-night experience backing rock 'n' roll legend Chuck Berry, who toured the country with just a bass player, picking up local drummers, keyboard players, and guitarists at his various stops. Brainiac backed Berry one night at Thumper's in Coon Rapids. Everybody knew his songs—and everyone who backed him quickly learned that Berry had some very rigid demands. "He disappears into the bathroom, and then he wants one of the bouncers to get him a young girl to blow him before the show," Inhofer said. "That's done, then he wants to meet the band. The bass player said, 'Watch Chuck's foot for the stops and starts; look to me and I'll tell you the key.' A, E, G, E-flat."

Inhofer added: "Dale's playing guitar. As soon as [Berry] hits the stage, he goes over to the roadies and says, 'Git that guitar player off the stage. Git that motherfucker off the stage!' He kicks him off the stage—he's too good. He kept me and Bernie and his bass player."

Berry played his hits, then announced that in his estimation they had played ten minutes over their contractual agreement, so he launched into his encore without leaving the stage. "He does his vamp, and says, 'Can we get the band's guitar player back onstage, please?'" Inhofer said. "Dale comes back up, Chuck takes off his guitar, and puts it in his case. From Thumper's you can see the dressing room, right over there on the side, and if the door's open, you can see all the way to the back door, and if that door's open, you can see all the way to the parking lot. Chuck walks out the back door. All the sudden you see the Mercury Monterey—we're still vamping. He opens the trunk, puts the guitar in, leaves the trunk open, gets in the passenger side. The bass player, in seeing this, plays doot-doot-dootley-doot! Bub-a-doo-doo! He puts his bass in its case, walks out the back door, puts his bass in the trunk, closes the trunk, gets in the driver's seat, and they're gone. Within a minute. There are 1,200 people chanting 'One more! One more!'"

————————

During a weeklong gig at Spolar's Bar in Hibbing, Brainiac's soundman, Doug Domisch, bought a one-watt laser at the Honeywell outlet store. "It was like a $20,000 laser, and he got it for eight hundred bucks," Inhofer said. "Now, a one-watt laser is about the size of my finger, and it's green. It will burn through things. It came with a refrigerator-sized unit, and you had to run water through it to cool it. He would only run it at quarter-power." They set up mirrors all over the club to catch the reflection of the laser and create the shape of a star with the crisscrossing beams. "The owner, Joe Spolar, sees Doug bend over and light his cigarette on the laser, and says, 'You're not runnin' that around my club, are ya?'"

But they were. Later in the evening, Domisch was looking at the laser gauge on the soundboard and noticed that it was spiking to dangerous levels. "Well, somebody, Joe or whoever, had turned off the water that was cooling it, and it was just about to blow up," Inhofer said. The water was quickly turned back on, and a rock 'n' roll tragedy was averted.

The band's ultimate demise came in a less spectacular fashion. "One night we're on break, and Bernie goes over to Dale and says, 'What are you doing? You're not moving around! If you were on a one-foot piece of asbestos and the stage caught on fire, you wouldn't even get burned!' That was it. Dale quit. We tried out some guitar players, but I don't think Bernie was into it, so we broke the band down."

————————

In 1980, Inhofer followed Bill Berg's lead and moved to Los Angeles with the Howard Arthur Band and jazz vocalist Corliss Dale. "They were moving to LA, and their keyboard player and bass player didn't want to go, so Doug [Nelson] and I hopped on. They were doing a version of *The Wiz*, dressed up as Dorothy and the Cowardly Lion, that shtick. We had a five-week stay at the Bonaventure." During that time, he and his wife, Carla, found a place to live and made what they thought might be a permanent move to the coast. Once established there, he got a referral from his friend John Farrar to audition for a band being fronted by ex–Herman's Hermits star Peter Noone. The band was called the Tremblers, shortened from Noone's preferred name, the Knee Tremblers. The group consisted of Noone on rhythm guitar and vocals, Inhofer on keyboards, Robert Williams on drums, George Conner on lead guitar, and Mark Browne on bass. According to the liner notes of their only album, several musicians provided "licks & tricks," including members of Tom Petty's Heartbreakers, Elton John's backing band, Daryl Dragon, Phil Seymour, and Dave Clark.

"So we're doing this new wave album, and Peter's saying, 'I want a band that can tell each other to fuck off onstage if we want to!'" Inhofer said. "And the first time I told him to fuck off, I got fired." That didn't happen until Inhofer had toured with the band for a couple of months and became the group's de facto road manager when the original road manager was fired for messing up an interview. "I spent my time setting up interviews two or three days in advance, doing the books, sending money back to the manager in LA, going to the bank, blah blah blah," Inhofer said. "I'd get to the gig with the soundman, talk to the crew there, and I'd say, 'Put a mic on Peter's amp, run the cord in back of it, and just coil it up. Don't plug it in.' 'Cause he sucked. So he had his amp going, and he's playing away, but nothing's coming out of the front. He never caught on."

There was a song on the album called "I Screamed Anne," on which there's an actual screaming part. "I was doing the scream because Peter couldn't do it live," Inhofer said. "I was doing the scream back from the keyboard spot. During rehearsal we all decided that I should do one of the guitar parts, because that guitar part is missing more than the keyboard part. So I'm up at the guitar mic next to Peter, and I'm scream-ing my part. Peter says, 'I think you should go back to your other micro-phone. Everyone's going to know it's you and not me.'"

Noone's ego would ultimately lead to Inhofer's exit from the Trem-blers. "I was road managing, and when I got back to town, I'm supposed to take the last of the proceeds into the accountant," Inhofer said.

> [Noone] had a deal going, like Tom Petty and the Heartbreakers, where the band split everything five ways. He took care of his own expenses. He wined and dined whatever radio people—that was all on him. He stayed in his own hotel and got the same per diem we did. I got back from one tour out east, and the accoun-tants are saying, "I can't give you a figure yet. We don't have Peter's American Express bill yet." "What do you mean, Peter's American Express bill? Peter's American Express bill isn't paid out of the pro-ceeds." "Well, yeah, it is."
>
> So I tell the band that. We're driving up the coast to San Fran-cisco to play a gig. Everybody's pissed. We're going to meet with Peter the next morning. I was Peter's right-hand man. The guitar player wanted to be Peter's right-hand man, so guess who didn't show up for the meeting? The guitar player. He told Peter. We're taping *Don Kirshner's Rock Concert*, and Peter comes in and he looks at me and says, "I don't see any reason you should still be in this band, after the shit you just caused." So I was out.

There's a Tremblers video easily found on YouTube made during a tap-ing of *The Midnight Special* with Wolfman Jack in which Noone delivers an impassioned, punky version of Elvis Costello's "Green Shirt," while Inhofer plays both keyboard and guitar and sings backup vocals. It's a tight, energetic performance, but the band never caught on.

———

Inhofer meanwhile began looking for another band. He read in *Rolling Stone* that Foreigner's keyboard player had quit, so he called Minneap-olis concert promoter Randy Levy for the phone number of Foreigner's management office. He dialed the number and spoke to a sweet-voiced receptionist named Mary Ann. "'Yeah, my name is Gregg Inhofer, I'm a keyboard player, and I read that what's his name is leaving the band, and I'd like to know about auditions."

"Oh, the boys are in the studio right now, and if you'd like to call back, I'll let you know when they're doing auditions."

He called back every few weeks and kept getting the same response. "They're not done yet, Gregg. Nice to talk with you." Feeling he at least had a little relationship going with Mary Ann, he called one day and got a gruff-voiced male. It was Bud Prager, manager of Foreigner, Megadeth, and Mountain. "I was talking with Mary Ann, and she was going to tell me when auditions were starting," Inhofer said.

"Well, just send a demo to our office and don't call here again." He sent a demo of his original material and received a call from Rick Wills, Foreigner's bass player. "Yeah, this is Rick Wills. We really like your stuff. Would you like to audition? Come out to New York." Inhofer flew to New York and met the band in SIR Studios in Chelsea. He'd charted every song from their three albums in notebooks and felt confident he could handle anything they threw at him.

"What would you like to do?"

"I'm ready to do anything off your first three albums."

"All right, let's do 'Cold As Ice.'" As soon as the band started the song, Inhofer realized that they were playing a half-step lower than the recorded version—in order to protect lead singer Lou Gramm's voice. Inhofer was momentarily thrown off.

"Oh, we tune it to E-flat on the road," he was told. "We tune everything down. Would you like to try another one?"

"Well, we can try this one."

"You're going to transpose it on the spot?"

"Sure."

"We've got a scholar here!" drummer Dennis Elliot yelled out.

"So I muddled through it," Inhofer said. "We did some other stuff. The drummer, the bass player, and I liked each other. We're feeding off each other. Rick Wills asked me, 'So what have you done?' That's where I lost the gig." Even though Inhofer had been a member of a number of successful bands over the past decade, not to mention touring with Olivia Newton-John and recording with Bob Dylan, he couldn't bring himself to tout his accomplishments:

> Because I don't know how to schmooze. I should have looked him in the eye and said, "You know what, Rick? It really doesn't matter what I've done, but what I can do. And what I can do is, when you say be in the lobby of the hotel at 5:30 a.m. to catch a flight, I'm there at 5:25." That's what I should have said. And I also played on *Blood on the Tracks*, Dylan's biggest record, I played with Olivia Newton-John, Peter Noone, blah blah blah. But I didn't.

Failing to land a job with an established hitmaking band, Inhofer decided to move back to the Twin Cities with his wife and new baby. He called his friend Bob Strength. "Bob, I'm moving back. Anybody need a keyboard player?"

"I'll fire my keyboard player." And he did.

The new band was called Parade. They were a contemporary cover band in clubs and hotels, playing whatever was on the Billboard Hot 100. That band morphed into Zerox in 1982, and in 1983, Inhofer went full-scale into the show-band business with a trio he called Triple Scale, as in charging three times whatever union scale was. It was Inhofer on keybass, John Della Selva on guitar, and Terry Ferguson on drums.

"This was beyond Top 40," Inhofer said. "This was multigenerational. We played everything from the '20s to the current songs. I was running the Yamaha Y-Cam system, a computer-driven thing where you'd program in stuff. I would program all the horns and everything else, push a button, and I'd go out front and do 'Sussudio' [by Phil Collins]. We had two robots. One would go out on the dance floor and dance with people—it looked like Cousin It. We had one that looked like a tiny R2D2, and you could program where you wanted it to go—just push the button. We'd get to the first day of a six-night gig, we'd program it to go to the bar and get you drinks, and it would come back." Where did they get the idea to do this kind of show? "A lot of drugs, a lot of alcohol," Inhofer said. "We were working five, six, seven nights a week. We hired the guitar player, the drummer, and I owned everything else—the truck, the lights, and the PA. We cleaned up, and we had a riot."

With all that money and all that fun, what could have induced Inhofer to leave for yet another band? The chance to play with former pro wrestler and future governor of Minnesota, Jesse "The Body" Ventura in 1985. "We wanted to play with Jesse," Inhofer said. "Bob Strength had done one show with Jesse at the Metrodome, and Jesse decided he wanted to go out on the road. His bass player didn't want to go, so I did. I played bass with him for about eight months." The band, called Soldiers of Fortune, consisted of Inhofer, Kid Skin Lizard on guitar (aka Mark Waryan), Waryan's wife Bev "Fingers" McKinney on guitar, Bob Strength on drums, and Ventura's wife, Terry, on tambourine and backup vocals. Inhofer recalled:

> Jesse was the lead shouter. We were doing stuff like "Eve of Destruction." He had a single out, "The Body Rules" and "Dancin' with Mr. V." We played outdoors at Woodley's Country Dam [Amery, Wisconsin]. It was rock 'n' wrestling. They had a wrestling match after we played. We'd be vamping this metal kind of stuff. He'd come walking out with his feather boa and his sunglasses. He'd come up to the mic and say, "All right, I'm not here to wrestle, and I'm not here to commentate on wrestling. I'm here to rock and roll, and if you don't like it, you can get the fuck out!" That's how he opened his show, a patriot out of Dale Carnegie. We traveled around for eight months on and off in an RV. Jesse would tell great stories. He was great—he's a loyal person. Bob and I have seen him when he's on his book tour. He sees you, and he says, "Hey, G.I., how you doin' man?" He's just a good guy.

When that gig ended, Inhofer was invited to play bass with Joey Molland, one of two remaining members of the band Badfinger. Molland had relocated to the Twin Cities. "I did one tour of Hawaii on bass with Joey," Inhofer said. "I loved it, but I couldn't keep doing it because he couldn't tell me how much work he had and how much the money was. I was raising kids, so couldn't continue to do it, even though I wanted to."

Inhofer had a brief stay in the Norm Stratton Band: "A minor-league baseball player who never made it to the bigs. He was a lead singer, not bad, not terrible, but a bleached blond, had that gorgeous look like David Hasselhoff. The women loved it." Then it was on to the Melvin James experience. "I recorded an album with Melvin on MCA," Inhofer said. "He was gonna be a big deal. They were putting a lot of money into him."

James was an Iowa native who had moved to Minneapolis and recorded a promising new wave album with his band the Crash Street Kids in 1982. Inhofer was hired to be in his backup band, along with drummer Kurt Barkdull and guitarist Donnie Paulson. MCA brought in famed producer Bill Szymczyk (producer for James Gang, the Eagles, J. Geils Band, B. B. King) to produce James at Metro Studios in Minneapolis. "Bill Szymczyk wanted to kill him by the time it was over," Inhofer said. "Melvin re-recorded the entire album because he wasn't happy with it."

After recording the album *The Passenger* with James in 1987, the three backing musicians were put on retainer by the label, and they began calling themselves Incognito. "Incognito was basically the Melvin James band, but he was not allowed to play," Inhofer said. "The record company wanted to put him on tour, and they wanted him to be a big deal. We would do two hours with just the three of us, without Melvin. We'd do cool commercial stuff like Genesis, the cooler cream of the crop. In the third-hour set, Melvin would come up and play his record, but we wouldn't introduce him. That's why we were Incognito."

The Melvin James project never panned out. According to Inhofer, James turned down a tour with REO Speedwagon because his manager said they were going to get an opening spot on the upcoming Rolling Stones tour. That never materialized. "What happened was Belinda Carlisle [lead singer of the Go-Go's] came out with her solo record on MCA," Inhofer said. "When that happened, all attention turned to her and away from Melvin. They spent a half-million on his record, and they just blew it off. He did some local stuff, then nothing."

After Melvin James failed to pan out, Incognito became the Fab Three, a commercial band that did weddings and parties. "We made so frickin' much money, I couldn't believe it sometimes," Inhofer said. "At weddings, we'd show up thirty minutes before a gig. We'd haul two PA speakers over people's heads at dinner. It was just a wonderful band. People loved us because we had so much fun. Everybody sang lead so we just went 'You sing, you sing.' During one of the songs, the next guy would look around, check the dance floor, and he would tell everybody during that song what the next song was going to be. Whoever was supposed to start it would start it. The band just went bing, bang, boom boom boom. During the dinner set we did swing versions of rock tunes. You could see grandma and grandpa tapping their feet, because it's swing, and the kids were going, 'That's the Stones! 'Start Me Up'!" To satisfy their artistic side, the Fab Three came up with yet another moniker during that time, the Original Band, or KGD—Kurt, Greg, and Donnie; or keyboard, guitar, and drums: "That band did all original material. We had everything: slogan, T-shirts, tickets, promo—we had everything except an audience."

At that point, Inhofer had already begun another project that would never lack an audience. He helped create the Teddy Bear Band, a group that continues to entertain young audiences at Twin Cities–area parties and gatherings to this day:

> I was taking my kids to an ECFE [Early Childhood and Family Education] program when they were little. A bass player I know [Dick Erickson] was also taking his kids at the same time. The director [Ron Gustafson] played a little acoustic guitar in college. At the end of the year, he asked us if we would be involved in a little musical program to raise money for ECFE. We said, "Sure." He had the idea. He went to see Raffi and noticed all these kids had Cabbage Patch dolls. There were ones who didn't. He thought, *What does every kid have? A teddy bear.* So he called it the Teddy Bear Band and encouraged the kids to bring their teddy bears.

The group came up with "Toss your bear up in the air" and other ways to engage the kids. At their first show, a number of day care providers were in attendance and asked how to book the group. "Ron didn't know anything about booking, but Dick did," Inhofer said. "Dick's been a bass player in bands around town for years. I was in his jazz band, his country band, and his beach band—we were called Sons of the Beach. He took over as the manager, he got gigs, and it took off. It was huge for a while. Every year we would do the State Fair. Five or six shows a day, every day of the fair, for seven years in a row, in my little pink Teddy Bear shorts and my little black-and-pink shirt."

Inhofer had to get used to a new kind of popularity that had nothing to do with the usual rock 'n' roll dream of stardom. Even years after he left the Teddy Bear Band, it followed him. "I was out to dinner with my wife, and I left something in the car," he said. "I walked out and there were three or four thirtyish young ladies, and one of them ran over to me and said, 'Were you in the Teddy Bear Band?' I said, 'Yes, I was.' 'My mom and I used to come and see you all the time.' So I went to my car, got one of my CDs, and said, 'Here, give that to your mom. This is what I'm doing now.'"

Inhofer's stint with the Teddy Bear Band lasted nearly ten years, until they landed a gig as the weeklong guest hosts of a local kiddie TV show. "For a week we were the emcees," he said. "We would do all these characters and skits. I was Maha-gregg. I was sitting cross-legged with a sheet. We did another one, Cowboy Roy—'Hey, kids, I'm Cowboy Roy.' It was goofy, but we were just introducing cartoons and doing skits in between. My wife, whom I met years later, had a videocassette of the Teddy Bear Band that her nephews used to watch all the time. When we got done with that show, I said, 'Hey, I'm going to represent us as actors.' I wanted to get into acting, but I didn't want Dick Erickson to represent me."

His timing didn't mesh with the other band members. They wanted him to come in as a full partner. Rather than make that commitment, Inhofer quit but asked for a buyout. "I told Dick, 'You can have all my songs and stuff,'" Inhofer recalled. "I had just gotten divorced, but I needed some money. I'm thinking maybe a $3,000 buyout, and I'll never come back and ask for anything. If something big had happened with the band, I would have sued his ass in a minute, because I had a lot to do with it. Maybe because I was drinking beer, but I was the one who was irreverent on stage. I was the Marx Brother. In the beginning, I was always getting the nervous looks from Ron and Dick, like, 'Heh, heh . . .' Then they realized people like that. That works. Then all of a sudden, Dick's getting one of those ZZ Top straps where the bass twirls around, and everybody's being goofy then."

When his wife, Annie, needed surgery, Inhofer realized he needed a day job to make ends meet, so he found work at Petters Warehouse. "We had a deal with [founder Tom Petters]: 'As long as you guys get twenty hours per week, we don't care when you come in,'" Inhofer remembered. "And if I had a session: 'Hey, Tom, I can't be in tomorrow.' No problem." Inhofer was offered the job of manager of Petters's Southdale store in Edina and took it for a year to get the health insurance. Then he had the opportunity to get involved in a recording studio in Maple Grove, so he quit Petters—with no hard feelings. "Tom Petters helped me get a line of credit so I could make that happen," Inhofer said. "We were called CBIG. His name was Pat Balder—PB, and I'm GI. We took those letters and we were going to be PBIG, but we decided, probably not."

After recording a couple of religious musicals written by Dick Wilson (the man who wrote the "We're Gonna Win, Twins" baseball theme song), some corporate commercial work, and a few videos, Balder asked Inhofer to leave. Inhofer continued to play in several bands, making good money at weddings and parties, but his drinking had reached the problem stage. He got sober in 1989, inspired by the writings of Nevada philosopher Frank R. Wallace.

Inhofer took a job with the *Star Tribune*, putting the weekend editions in racks at fifty stores around town. He continued to play in several bands. Steve Millar and Diamondhead were "doing talent shows once a week at a casino down in Southwest Minnesota: you had to learn a bunch of stuff to back up the talent people." Inhofer also played with the Doug Maynard band. Maynard was a gravelly voiced R&B singer whom Inhofer had known since he played with Stan Kipper in the

Marauders in the late 1960s. But tragedy struck in 1991 when Maynard committed suicide. Maynard's band kept playing, changing its name to Passage, as Inhofer assumed the role of lead singer. Passage spawned an offshoot trio called King Bee, featuring Inhofer on keybass and organ, Max Santiago on drums, and Bobby Schnitzer on guitar. They would sometimes add a sax player, one of which was Kathy Jensen, who as a member of the Hornheads with her husband, Dave, toured and recorded with Prince's New Power Generation band in the early '90s. Inhofer also worked with the Jensens in the Brian Kinney Band—"a wedding and events band, corporate stuff."

———————

Inhofer had always nurtured a love of acting, comedy, and doing impressions, which is why his next band, White Boy Blues, was one of his favorites:

> I loved that band. We played the British Blues invasion of the '60s and '70s. White Boy Blues is what all the old blues artists used to call the British blues players, like Clapton and Beck. I played mostly guitar, as my alter ego, Nigel Underhill. Nigel's thing was he was my separated-at-birth identical twin. We were separated in London. I was raised by a German couple from Minnesota, he was raised by a sheep farmer thirty kilometers south of Sussex. As Nigel would say [in British accent], "Yes, get in a van, start smoking thirty kilos of pot, and when you're done, you'll be in Sussex." When his parents died, he discovered papers about his adoption. He went to the London hospital he was found at and found he had a twin. So he went to Minnesota to find his long-lost twin, which was me. I would play these gigs, and I would never drop character. Nigel grew up with all the greats, Eric Clapton, Jeff Beck. He was doing gigs, but he just never made it.
>
> One of [Nigel's] stories [with accent]: "Yes, I remember playing the Rusty Nail; it was a seven-band bill. I believe I was in the seventh band on the bill. I was in the basement, and then Eric Clapton

said eight words to me that I've never forgotten: 'Nigel, pop out and get me some smokes.' I've never forgotten that."

Band members included old friend Bob Strength on drums, who billed himself as Robert Strong, and Marie Mead on bass, who changed her name to Petula East. "Petula East's real name was Eastman, but she dropped the -man when her sister stole her boyfriend, Paul," Inhofer said. "Randy Anderson was on guitar. That was his real name. As Nigel said, 'With a name like Randy, why would you change it?'"

Inhofer was simultaneously playing as a solo act (as himself), and one night at Famous Dave's in uptown Minneapolis his two personas came together. "I had just played there on a Tuesday with White Boy Blues," Inhofer said. "There was a mother and daughter celebrating their birthday. Nigel of course was being Nigel. They just loved him. I'm there on Friday on break. The woman who was there on Tuesday came up to me and starts talking to me about Tuesday, about Nigel, and I'm looking at her kind of confused, and finally I said, 'Oh, you must be referring to my brother Nigel.' She said, 'Oh, you must tell the story.' I went and told the story to her table. And they bought it. That whole Nigel thing was being able to go up to a table of bikers or old people, and they would be equally enamored. It was the accent or something. That was my onstage patter. People that didn't know me bought it, and people who did didn't."

As much as he loved the character of Nigel and playing the blues, the band lasted only a year or so. "We didn't get a lot of work." As a sideman, however, he was always in demand. When singer-songwriter Shawn Phillips staged his twenty-fifth anniversary concert at Minneapolis's Orchestra Hall in October 1995, Inhofer was recruited to be in the band. Phillips was a Texas native but adopted the Twin Cities as a second home when KQRS began playing his records in the early '70s, causing his career to take off.

"Peter Robinson, the keyboard player, flew in from England and Paul Buckmaster, the cellist, was supposed to fly in because they had a special song that the three of them did that was huge to his following," Inhofer said. "People came from Canada, they came from everywhere, to that show. At the last minute, Paul Buckmaster couldn't make it. Some genius in the band said, 'Oh, hell, I'm sure Inhofer has a cello-into-synthesizers somewhere. You could just play it.' Like God, c'mon, we're talking a real cello here, you know? So, I pull up a cello sound. It's simple stuff—you know, it's just play in the bottom end. They said, 'Okay.' So that moment onstage when the band left and I was left out there with Peter Robinson and Shawn Phillips, playing a synthesized cello, was powerful because the audience was hanging on every word," he said.

"And that's right up there with playing on [Dylan's album]." From that point, Inhofer began concentrating on writing songs and developing a solo career. But his experience with *Blood on the Tracks* was not over yet. Far from it.

9

"Blown Out on the Trail"

FOUR OF THE SIX MINNESOTA MUSICIANS WHO GRACED THE
Blood on the Tracks album had extensive experience either performing, recording, or both, but the résumés for Peter Ostroushko and Chris Weber were comparatively thin when the sessions were held. Ostroushko was at the very beginning of a career that would eventually see him become a world-renowned mandolin player. He had been tapped to appear on the first season of Garrison Keillor's *A Prairie Home Companion* radio show just months before the Dylan session, along with his guitar-playing partner Dakota Dave Hull. Yet he was already exhibiting a confidence—almost a fearlessness—that belied his twenty-one years. He sharpened his chops by playing constantly. "Back in those days I loved to play music more than anything else in life," he said on a podcast recorded in 2019. "If someone asked me to play with them, I would play with them at the drop of a hat. At all the get-togethers that would happen at the Extempore during the week, I would be there, and I would play with everybody."

He began writing songs, starting with "Hey, Big Fat Mama," which he called "a love song for overweight people," because he'd struggled with his weight throughout his school years. "I don't think 'Hey, Big Fat Mama' was going to displace 'The Times They Are A-Changing' anytime soon, but it was a start for me. It strikes me that Becky [Reimer], Dave, and I felt the need to be able to express ourselves through music and write our own music," Ostroushko said. "The same was true with basically everybody I knew in the West Bank at the time who were playing in the coffeehouses. Everyone was always playing the latest song that they wrote. Maybe it was because we came from the state that Bob Dylan came from."

His partnership with Hull continued through the first season of *Prairie Home*, but in June 1975 Ostroushko broke up the duo because he wanted to put his energies into mandolin playing and to "fulfill my destiny of becoming a fiddler." Soon thereafter he caught a performance by the duo of Robin and Linda Williams, visiting the New Riverside Cafe from their home state of Virginia. He enjoyed their music so much that he approached them afterward and said he'd like to play fiddle with them. They agreed and were impressed with Ostroushko's skill. He was invited to play on their first album, recorded in the Twin Cities with Paul Martinson engineering. Then they called him a few weeks later and asked him to go on the road with them. Ostroushko quickly agreed and took a train to Virginia to meet up with them. They embarked on a tour of college coffeehouses around the country and ended up playing Stout State College in Menominee, Wisconsin. Ostroushko called Keillor and suggested he might want to make the hour-long drive from St. Paul to Stout to check out their act. Keillor did so and liked the trio so much that he booked them on his next show. That began a long association between *Prairie Home* and the Williams duo—while Ostroushko solidified a position on the show that would last forty years and result in his being named the show's musical director.

"We hired him in the Sky Blue Water Boys when he got off the road with Robin and Linda," Becky Reimer Thompson said. "He played with us for a little over a year. That was amazing to have three lead instruments in that band. I still do some of his arrangements on some of those songs because they were incredible. We played at Summer Fest in Milwaukee. One year we opened for Doug Kershaw. We did 'Foggy Mountain Breakdown,' of course, and the way Peter had arranged it was an incredible arrangement. Doug stole it and put it out on his record. Playing with him was a joy."

When *A Prairie Home Companion* was picked up by National Public Radio in 1980 for coast-to-coast distribution, Ostroushko became a permanent cast member. Becky Thompson performed many times on the show, almost always with Ostroushko. "Every time I was on, we did a trio, unless they called me at the spur of the moment," she said. "Most of the time it was Peter, Cal Hand, and I, up until 1984. It must have been ten years. I told Garrison I thought that was an amazing thing for him to get Peter. That was huge. Garrison had a lot of respect and admiration and caring for Peter."

By then, Ostroushko was a veteran recording artist, guesting on many albums by folk and country artists. The first album featuring his own name was 1979's *Dixie Highway Sign*, billed as Robin and Linda Williams with Peter Ostroushko. In 1983, he was again a billed fiddle and mandolin player on the bluegrass album *Scott Alarik and the New Prairie Ramblers featuring Peter Ostroushko*.

His solo debut was released on Rounder Records in 1985, titled *Peter Ostroushko with the Sluz Duz Orchestra—Slüz Düz Music (Original American Dance Tunes with an Old World Flavor)*. *Slüz düz* was a Ukrainian expression meaning "over the edge" or "off his rocker." A year later he released *Down the Streets of My Neighborhood*, which included Hank Williams's "Hey, Good Lookin'" sung in Ukrainian. He switched labels to St. Paul–based Red House Records for his third album, *Peter Ostroushko Presents the Mando Boys*, with a cover shot of four fez-topped, sunglasses-wearing mandolin players purportedly named Maxim, Habib, Maurice, and Sonny—actually Ostroushko, Dick Nunneley, Joe Trimbach, and John Niemann.

That same year, Ostroushko paired up with concertina player Bertram Levy to record *First Generation* on the Flying Fish label. Then he returned to Red House to make *Buddies of Swing*, featuring a large group of guest musicians including *Prairie Home* pianist Butch Thompson and fiddler Johnny Gimble from Bob Wills and the Texas Playboys. His 1989 album *Blue Mesa* featured guest appearances by Norman and Nancy Blake, and in 1991 Ostroushko paired up with guitarist Dean Magraw to record *Duo*.

Ostroushko's old singing partner, Becky Reimer Thompson, meanwhile was going back and forth to Nashville, working with songwriter Dennis Morgan, when she contracted rheumatoid arthritis. "We were thinking about moving, and all of a sudden I got hit with that," she said. "I couldn't play anymore. For about a year I was completely out of touch with anybody, trying to get some drug that actually would lessen the pain. We had moved to Albert Lea to cut expenses and make my life a little easier with my kids and husband. Peter came down to Albert Lea and played a concert with me. That must have been in 1990. Then in 1994 we did the street dance for Garrison. Chet Atkins opened, and then Peter came on with us."

The album Ostroushko is best remembered for is *Heart of the Heartland*, released in 1995 and featured as theme music for Ken Burns's PBS film *Lewis and Clark*. He followed that with the semipolitical *Pilgrims on the Heart Road* in 1997 and the eclectic *Sacred Heart* in 2000.

After all his collaborations with folk, bluegrass, jazz, and country artists, he was soon to reunite with the musicians who were there at the start of his recording career.

———————

Following his unexpected role in the making of *Blood on the Tracks*, Chris Weber returned to running the Podium guitar shop in Dinkytown. Not only did he have the satisfaction of playing on the historic session; he'd sold the Martin 00-42 to Dylan.

"Bob scratched it," Vanessa Weber said. "He did end up buying it. We were paid—I don't know if [Mark] Zelenovich sent $1000, but [Dylan] didn't have a personal check. Chris got paid either in cash or check. [Dylan] ended up giving it to an out-of-luck friend. I don't think he kept it very long. We did see him later in concert, and he didn't play it. I think he had decided he wasn't interested in it. It wasn't the guitar he had—that's what was missing. It wasn't the same."

Amanda Weber was born a month later, just about the time *Blood on the Tracks* was released. "People were coming down to the store saying, 'Hey, congratulations,' and Chris would say, 'Yeah, she's seven pounds, four ounces,'" Vanessa said. "What are we congratulating, an album or a kid?"

Upon the release of *Blood on the Tracks*, Weber was interviewed a number of times by local journalists, all of whom brought up the fact that the Minneapolis guys didn't get their names on the album. Vanessa said the lack of credit for the Dylan sessions was a sore point for Chris.

"At first you couldn't prove it—that it was him playing on it," she said. "People had to take his word for it till the Internet came along. That was the only way, except for a few articles, *Rolling Stone*, and that kind of thing. It would have benefited Gregg Inhofer so much. It would have been so beneficial for him if they knew that was him, because he was really good."

There were casual mentions by Dylan at the end of the Minneapolis sessions that he was looking for musicians to accompany him on the road, but Bill Berg was headed for California and Billy Peterson was not going to leave town with a young family at home. Same with Weber. "Dylan showed interest in Chris traveling with him, but we had just bought the Podium, we just had a kid, and he wasn't going on the road," Vanessa said. "He always felt he made the right choice. If he had gone, I'd have one kid and a different husband."

Instead of pursuing rock 'n' roll dreams, Weber settled down to the day-to-day business of running a guitar shop. The Podium lasted another decade, but increased competition became too much to overcome. "We couldn't maintain the business once Guitar Center came to town," Vanessa said. "We had to do something else. We gave up the store in 1985. We basically ended up losing everything. We had two teenagers and a baby, so the house went to the bank. My parents took out a loan, and we assumed that. After we lost the Podium, it was a terrible blow for him." Vanessa admits that Weber had moments when he wondered what might have happened if he'd pursued his own musical career. "It did go through his mind a few times," she said. "'If I'd gone off with Dylan, I'd have made money instead of scrambling for eleven years to make it work.' He closed the door on that."

The Webers moved to Minnetonka and became realtors, which turned the family fortunes around. "He was great at it," Vanessa said. "He knew how to talk to people. We ended up doing very well. We just did real estate for twenty years. We had a home office; I was the broker. We didn't have any company rules. I had gotten a great education in purchase agreements and knew all the ins and outs before I got my broker's license."

In Minnetonka, Weber played with a group of guys—Dick Chronic,

Morrie Lazarus, and Milton "Soupy" Schindler—who called themselves Quick Grits. "The same guys would come over every Saturday," Vanessa said. "They recorded themselves, and he'd play with these guys whenever possible, but one of the members—a lawyer—didn't want to perform. [Chris] should have looked for other people who wanted to perform. We had to work, so he never really pursued it. It was frustrating for him. He would have loved to perform."

Weber initially followed Dylan's career after *Blood on the Tracks* closely, buying every one of his albums as soon as it was released. But after losing his guitar shop, Weber struggled to stay interested. "He just didn't listen to music much for a while after we moved out of Minneapolis," Vanessa said. "Music was sort of a sore point. It was really painful losing the Podium. Getting together with his friends and playing was therapeutic. He didn't do that for a while, and we didn't run out and buy albums. None of the albums were really interesting to him. His next love would have been going out and performing, but he couldn't get that to happen."

It would take a reunion with his fellow *Blood on the Tracks* bandmates to rekindle Weber's musical fire.

———

"It was an accident of nature," Kevin Odegard said of the Dylan sessions. "I think of the Yiddish word *beshert*—it was meant to be. It was destined to be. That thing fell together like a rainstorm out of the sky. You just looked up and you were wet. I didn't think anybody ran that show. It happened, it came out of the ether, because of the clarity and peacefulness that were around Bob at that moment. It happened in the perfect circumstance for us to be talking about it today."

Odegard actually stayed in touch with Dylan for a brief period following *Blood on the Tracks*. In the summer of 1975, Odegard was hired to play a wedding at Camp TEKO, a Jewish summer camp on Lake Minnetonka. The bride and groom were friends of the Zimmermans, and during Odegard's performance, Dylan and his lifelong pal from Duluth, Louie Kemp, pulled up in a GMC motorhome. "I was playing with a steel player I brought with me named Mark Lee," Odegard said. "We had a battery-powered amp for him, and we sat out there in the middle of the pasture at this wedding. Bob was ten feet in front of me with his back to me, and I'm singing 'Forever Young' from his previous album *Planet Waves*. He said, 'Thank you,' and 'Good job,' and he gave me his very famous limp handshake. Louie did a little bit more of the talking; it was pleasant."

Following that meeting, Dylan agreed to have Odegard cut a demo of a song called "Nobody 'cept You," an outtake from the *Planet Waves* sessions. Dylan wanted country singer Johnny Rodriguez to record the song, but he also wanted a demo version that wouldn't be bootlegged, like everything else Dylan recorded. So Odegard cut it at Sound 80's small recording room in the IDS building in downtown Minneapolis. Rodriguez never recorded the song, but—as Dylan hoped—there was no rush to bootleg Odegard's version either. "The phone rang many more times," Odegard said. "I did several things for Bob and David. I worked out at the farm and at the IDS vocal booth."

Odegard also kept his brakeman job on the Chicago & Northwestern railroad and continued to perform with his KO Band. In 1975, Owen Husney got Odegard another leave of absence from the railroad to record his second solo album, *Silver Lining*. The album was recorded at ASI Studios in Minneapolis and produced by David Rivkin, with an assist from David Zimmerman. Billy Peterson played bass on several cuts, along with guest appearances by Bob Strength, Tony Glover, Mark Lee, and old friends Steve DeLapp, Billy Hallquist, and Bobby Rivkin.

It was around this time that Odegard broke up with Nancy Bundt. "He went to go fishing in Mexico with his buddy," Bundt recalled. "I wanted to go and he said, 'No, you don't take your girlfriend.' I was stubborn, too, so I went to Mexico by myself and didn't come back for months. Then we kind of broke up. We stayed friends."

Odegard took to the road to promote *Silver Lining*, but the KO Band "blew up in Owen Husney's office," in 1977, Odegard said. "I got fired for misbehaving." In 1978, Odegard married Mindy Isaacs at the Calhoun Beach Club in uptown Minneapolis and converted to Judaism. "It all started when my mother accidentally sent me to a Jewish Boy Scout camp. The people I gravitated toward were all Jewish. The Minneapolis music scene had a large Jewish contingent, who were very active and inspirational, including on the distribution end. That is something that I still embrace and still honor. And I still observe."

With the demise of his band, Odegard and his bride tricked out a van with a doggie window, put their two dogs inside, and drove to Los Angeles. He had landed a job working for Brendan Cahill at Colgems, a record label created for the Monkees in 1966 that was a joint venture between Screen Gems, the television division of Columbia Pictures, and RCA Victor. "Brendan was involved with the Monkees," Odegard said. "They were over, but Colgems existed, and the publishing entity was on the Columbia lot. I was going to be a demo singer. I arrived on a small stipend, but then David Begelman was ousted as head of Columbia Pictures, and all budgets were dropped, including me."

Nevertheless, the Odegards found a house in Santa Monica, and Odegard took a job as a delivery driver for graphic paste-up artists in downtown LA. "I never was afraid to work, and I was always working transportation jobs." After three or four years of driving, Odegard stumbled into an intern position at the American Guild of Authors and Composers (AGAC) at 6363 Sunset Boulevard in Los Angeles. "I volunteered," he said. "I struck a vein of overlooked gold, working for every living survivor of the Great American Songbook. The people I met at AGAC were the people who represented Irving Berlin, George Gershwin, Patti Andrews, Burt Bacharach, and newer composers like David Foster."

Every day on his way into the office, Odegard would walk into the building, look to his right, and see Chuck Berry sitting on a stool in the diner. "He's a prickly guy, but over time he became familiar with my face," Odegard said. "Eventually he waved me in for nonsense chatter and shop talk. Eventually he told me why he wasn't a member. 'I've been screwed by every music publishing company in the business. Ever heard 'Surfin' U.S.A.' [by the Beach Boys]? Ever heard 'Come Together' [by the Beatles]? You see, when you join AGAC they tithe from every song you write; they take a percentage of your earnings. Why should I give up a piece for them to collect my royalties? I have my own way of doing things. Ask anybody.'"

The older composers were a bit more trusting. Sammy Cahn, lyricist for such standards as "Time After Time," "It's Magic," "Let It Snow," and Frank Sinatra's "Come Fly with Me," took Odegard under his wing and hired him as his driver. Odegard was introduced to all of Cahn's friends as he drove the legendary songwriter around town for errands and medical appointments. "Best job I ever had," Odegard said.

> We'd start the day at his home and light out in his black Chrysler LeBaron convertible. He was seventy, and the days of the Rat Pack were gone. They were dying off, but he kept his own name in the game. Sammy Cahn was a hustler and still ambitious. At 4 p.m., we'd pull up to the Hillcrest Country Club, where we'd find Milton Berle, Mel Brooks, Sid Caesar, Henny Youngman, Alan King, Mel Tormé, Hal Kantor, and a rotating cast of looney luminaries. They'd regale each other with outrageous material they could never use on TV, smoke cigars, drink coffee, and work the room. Everybody was still hustling. This was 1982—Hillcrest Country Club was the only Jewish country club in LA. If you were sitting at this table drinking coffee and not paying attention, Uncle Milty was ready to pounce on your faux pas: "Are we boring you, sire?" I never saw anyone order a cocktail. Cigars and coffee provided enough fuel. The irreverent ghost of Groucho Marx hovered over the room.

Odegard and Cahn were allowed one road trip by Cahn's wife, Tita: to the desert town of Rancho Mirage to visit Cahn's old songwriting partner, pianist Jimmy Van Heusen. "Sammy missed his best collaborator," Odegard said. "We arrived at Jimmy and Bobbe's [Bobbe Brock, Van Heusen's wife] to find a bedridden Van Heusen, following a stroke or two. He was unable to speak, but he smiled. But their glory days were gone forever. Sammy said not a word on the drive back. Tita looked at us at the door as if to say, 'You can never go home again, boys.'"

In 1982, Odegard received a call from LA music attorney Al Schlesinger, who told him about a songwriter organization called Studio Recording Services that was going under. Schlesinger wanted SRS to be a service for new songwriters, but the group had run out of funding. "As I read through the information, I recognized a name—Billy

James, who was once the Byrds' publicist," Odegard said. "That got my attention. I also recognized Doug Field, Bruce Kaplan, Pete Luboff, Elsa Paladino—names I'd read about in the trades at Shinders in Minneapolis. I went back home to Minneapolis after that for a family celebration. I consulted the Odegard's most trusted family friend, Dr. Al Zelickson, who listened to me and offered advice. He said, 'Was it a train wreck or an opportunity to do what I could?' I rolled the dice of running my own shop."

For no salary, Odegard became head of the newly named National Academy of Songwriters. At NAS's first meeting, he remembered the words of Chuck Berry and tried to structure the new service in a way that would establish trust among the songwriters who felt they'd been ripped off. "We got together in a conference room at A&M Records," Odegard said.

> The Police [with A&M] were the hottest group on the planet at that time. I remember the Santa Ana winds blowing really hot across La Brea Avenue. I had shown up early. I switched off the air conditioning and it was bloody scorching by the time we started. We opened our door and had a meeting with Schlesinger, the Luboffs, and other benefactors. We gathered together a list of the most successful songwriters who lived in LA. Barry Mann, Cynthia Weil, John Bettis, Gerry Goffin—I stood and made a case for the new guild. We were in a climate when digital and other new issues were popping up almost every day. We would instead somehow fundraise, but we had no freaking idea how we would fundraise— music, TV, film, stage? I was proposing in vague terms that we would become a visible presence, a positive voice for songwriters. I kept it short and headed to the thermostat. The Antons held up a check for $25,000 and implored everyone in the room with means to do the same. For the most part, they did.

Soliciting checks from successful industry people was not going to be enough to keep NAS going. Their main fundraising tool was an annual show called *Salute to the American Songwriter*. "In our first year, none other than Brian Wilson showed up," Odegard said. "The big reveal during the show was the introduction of the songwriters in attendance. It was a trick. It opened in 1987 with a warbling, barely audible Burt Bacharach singing 'On My Own.' He handed the song off to Carole Bayer Sager, who forgot the lyrics. Cue Michael McDonald, who came out from backstage and picked it up. The crowd went wild—standing ovation. It was happening."

NAS lobbied for better copyright protection, taught the craft and business of songwriting, offered marketing advice, and published a magazine called *SongTalk* that featured interviews with songwriters including Paul McCartney, Madonna, and Bob Dylan. Odegard got a chance to talk to Dylan in 1986 at an ASCAP party in Los Angeles, attended by stars including Neil Young, Liz Taylor, and Chrissie Hynde. "He gave me a handshake and a few words of encouragement," Odegard said.

The annual *Salute* featured Carole King, Jackson Browne, Stevie Wonder, Los Lobos, Willie Dixon ("he had a grand mal seizure the night he played"), Stephen Stills ("he came off his boat to do a set"), Michael Bolton, Melissa Manchester, Stephen Bishop, and Jimmy Webb, among many others. Brian Wilson came back for a second appearance. "From the old days, we had Jay Livingston and Ray Evans," Odegard said. "Sammy Fain was one of my favorites. He wrote 'I'll Be Seeing You' and 'Love Is a Many Splendored Thing.' Hearing 'I'll Be Seeing You,' I cried—I stood in the wings and wept. The luck we had to put this group of writers and entertainers together—Roger McGuinn, who has been a dear friend since then; Billy Davis and Marilyn McCoo, Roger Miller, Diane Warren, Steve Cropper, Lamont Dozier."

In 1988, the fourth annual *Salute* was televised on VH1 and Showtime. "Hollywood was smiling on me," Odegard said.

It was good, and yet it was a busy time. It took all of my time. I was always going to be in Minnesota. The Midwestern values were my stock and trade. The songwriters trusted me. Many of them were migrants. Very few came from LA. Hollywood is just a ramshackle temporary encampment carved into the brush by the nine movie moguls—Eastern Europeans that came to create Hollywood.

Eventually what began as a string of movie lots became America's largest metropolis. Through fires, floods, and riots in LA, I kept in touch with Minnesota friends and family. Minnesotans were always welcome in my office. I had an inner sanctum, guarded by a fiercely loyal assistant. It was always a given that Elvis could be holding on Line 2, but whenever somebody from home called, I picked up. Paul Metsa. Barry Thomas Goldberg. Bobby Rivkin.

Bobby Rivkin, my camp buddy and drummer, who'd been plucked from obscurity, was the biggest fucking rock star drummer on planet Earth. You can't argue with that. I was invited to Prince's video shoots and parties—now Bobby's at the top of the show biz world. His success reaffirmed my belief in him.

It was at one of Prince's parties that Odegard met his first Beatle, Ringo Starr. "From 1964, I was on the hunt to meet all four," Odegard said. "Ringo was diminutive but loaded with charisma. It had been twenty years earlier, but he was still a Beatle to me. He was very nice, very kind. The second Beatle I didn't meet was John Lennon, but I saw him more than once in a neighborhood sushi restaurant on Pico. I didn't want to bother him, knowing his cutting wit. He deserved a small semblance of dignity. Bob [Dylan] had schooled me in the rules of engagement—you speak when you're spoken to." Odegard met his next Beatle, Paul McCartney, at a BMI function. "He's an extrovert like Ringo," Odegard said. "He loves his fans. So far, I'm batting a thousand, exceeding every expectation."

Odegard left NAS (which later merged with the Songwriters Guild of America) in 1989 for a job representing the Screen Gems catalogues. "The phone rang off the hook at that place for licensing deals," Odegard said. "As a publisher, I became a night owl. I was out every night at showcases, every single Hollywood Bowl concert—Tina Turner, Bruce Hornsby, the Moodys, Yanni from Minneapolis, now a New Age pop star, who was with Linda Evans. I watched the Pogues prove for one night that alcohol works miracles for a little while. Shane MacGowan was out of his mind drunk."

At the Billboard Music Awards in December 1992, Odegard was

backstage at the Universal Amphitheater when he felt a nudge on his left shoulder. It was Tom Petty handing him a joint, holding his breath, and nodding.

> I took a toke, coughed a little bit, and turned to my right to see George Harrison. The ash on the end of the joint broke off and fluttered downward to George's knee. I had to think fast. George had not yet gone onstage—I was going to be the one to put a hole in his slacks? This was no way to meet my third and favorite Beatle. Across the room, Jeff Lynne caught my eye and made a frantic swatting motion. I took the cue and swept the offending ember from the Beatle's dungarees. He took the signal and I introduced myself just before he went to get his award. I never saw him again. I loved everything he stood for. I've done an extensive study of George Harrison. He hated the music business, and like me, he was very shy, but he wasn't the quiet Beatle. That was made up by [publicist] Derek Taylor. He would talk your ear off. I was like Forrest Gump. I could push a button and turn it on. That's why I loved George so much.

There was one famous person in Hollywood that Odegard was not eager to talk to: Phil Ramone, the New York record producer and engineer whose work Odegard and his friends partially redid during the Minneapolis *Blood on the Tracks* sessions. "I stayed a million miles away from him in LA," Odegard said. "The only time I brought up Dylan was with a newspaper reporter. If you say something like that in Los Angeles, it follows you around and you never talk about anything else. Phil and I did several symposiums. I was cautious never to broach the subject."

Odegard expanded on his relations with Ramone to author Clinton Heylin in 2018. "Phil and I rubbed shoulders often in the eighties and early nineties, not always happily," Odegard said. "Rarely, if ever, did we discuss *Blood on the Tracks* directly. When it did come up, I was careful to focus on his brilliant career and redirect the discussion away from [the album] as soon as possible. It was always a sore spot for Phil. I knew that his blood pressure would spike if it came up, and he'd clam up around me to avoid bashing me outright for participating in the despoiling of his Dylan legacy. *Blood on the Tracks* was a project about which he was rightfully proud and righteously pissed off for the rest of his life."

Odegard said he took pains while in Los Angeles not to talk about Dylan because he didn't want to get stereotyped as a Dylan sideman. "Because then you're an out-of-work Dylan sideman," he said. "If you get pigeonholed, like a character actor, that's what you remain." For much the same reason, Odegard never tried to resume his music career after moving to Los Angeles. "I didn't cross the line," he said. "There was a line between being ethical and being opportunistic. Should I have? Of course I should have. Did I get rich in the music business? No, but I'm not crying in my beer. I've had a gifted life. Dozier, Cropper—my big brothers—none of that would have been possible if I'd been trying to get hooked up with my songwriting. I couldn't be that guy. I was only the custodian, not the creator."

Odegard did have a recording studio and kept working on his craft—in his attic. "I had Sneaky Pete [Kleinow, of the Flying Burrito Brothers] on pedal steel, Rowland Salley of Chris Isaak's band on bass," he said. "Yes, privately, I had a studio."

After 1992, Odegard said he lost the fire in the belly he'd had for Hollywood. "I was right that songwriters were the heart of the business, but wrong about almost everything else," he said. "Music became free, and compensation was narrowed down to the elite, proven hitmakers. New aspiring songwriters were left for dead. Because I'd lost the fire, and lyrics had degenerated, dream jobs from that point forward pretty much evaporated. I'd done some good work promoting America's lesser-known songwriters, advocating for rights and earnings, but I ended up doing very little to protect young songwriters."

A decade later, he ran into singer Judy Collins, who remembered his work in Los Angeles and posed a blunt question. "What happened to you?" she asked. "Why did you leave lesser songwriters high and dry?"

"I ran out of time," Odegard said, tears welling up. "I forgot to take care of myself and my family. I failed as a family man." That failure had yet to transpire as Odegard and his family headed back to Minnesota through the Rocky Mountains on July 4, 1994. "I was returning with a U-Haul trailer loaded with the spoils of failure—plaques and awards that meant nothing anymore," Odegard said. "My dreams-come-true framework became a waking, rolling nightmare. I wondered what would become of me. It had taken sixteen years for my magic carpet ride to crash and burn." He drove down North Main Street in Durango, Colorado, on that Independence Day and was welcomed by a couple dressed in red, white, and blue. They asked him to roll down his window. "North Main is closed, but you can be in the parade," they told him. "We have a sign prepared for your U-Haul."

Down the street, all the trailers and vans were plastered with signs that said, "Leaving Dodge." Odegard joined the parade, waving to families on the sidewalk. "The fires, the floods, the earthquakes fell behind me," he said. "All us refugees were parading down North Main Street in Durango, heading back to peace and quiet all across America."

What Odegard was actually heading back to was another transportation job, driving and training other drivers for Metro Mobility. Not too long after he started there, he noticed a request for proposals on his boss's desk. "In Hollywood I learned how to read upside down," he said. "I had to know what it was." It was a proposal to start Minneapolis River City Trolley, a sightseeing service with entertainment. He came up with a proposal of his own and soon was back in show business. He set to work writing and creating a script and hired a crew of drivers and musicians: "Anybody who could perform a script, pass a drug test, and was my friend got to be a trolley driver."

One Sunday he stopped his trolley on Main Street and heard a familiar voice with a Liverpudlian accent: Ringo Starr. He greeted the ex-Beatle with a firm handshake and reminded him of their meeting at one of Prince's parties in Los Angeles. "I do remember the party, but I don't remember you," Ringo said with a laugh. Odegard recalls feeling on top of the world after his second meeting with Ringo.

Then his world started to unravel again:

"In the middle of all this crazy, happy period, my brother Stephen died," Odegard said. "He was a brilliant guy, an Eastern European scholar and trumpeter. He had installed a stereo system in our house and his record collection was immense. He was also rich and also very dark. He knew the intimate details of all the most famous composers. He regaled me with tales of Mendelsohn, Wagner, Schumann. Wilhelm Furtwängler—he'd pronounce that name in our bedroom till I laughed. Upstairs in my house, my mother would for hours on end play Chopin and Schubert, but down in the catacombs it was serious business, playing trumpet, Handel, and Vivaldi. His greatest fascination was Mahler. He had an IQ north of 160, but his life ended tragically at fifty. That left a mark."

It would get worse. He was at work in 1999 when he got a call from his mother. He thought she was inviting him to lunch, but instead she was calling to tell him she'd gotten a terminal diagnosis: inflammation of the lungs. They would meet for lunch at his dad's house ("the best part of both of our days"), just a few minutes away from his workplace. Then he got another phone call. "I thought she was inviting me to lunch, but she'd taken ill at the Minikahda Club," Odegard said. "I showed up at Methodist Hospital too late to say goodbye. This left me inconsolable for years. She was my greatest fan and best friend. Many people have experienced this shock when a loved one passes. It's always a shock. You plan, you brace yourself, but no one and nothing can replace your brother and mother. I was off the map again, headed for more rocky shoals."

10

"Hear Me Singing through These Tears"

One of us (Metsa) played a part in the reunion of the Minneapolis
studio band. In the narrative describing these efforts,
the first-person pronoun is Paul.

KEVIN ODEGARD'S KO BAND STAGED A REUNION IN 2000 AT
Mayslack's, a self-proclaimed dive bar in northeast Minneapolis. The
event was successful and inspired me to attempt to reunite the original
Blood on the Tracks studio band for a one-night concert. (I am a native of
Virginia, Minnesota, and have been a Bob Dylan fan from my earliest
days.) Bob Dylan turned sixty on May 24, 2001. May 23 was chosen as
the date of the celebration, and First Avenue, the downtown Minneapolis music club made famous by Prince in *Purple Rain*, was chosen as the
venue for what came to be called the Million Dollar Bash.

I almost went to Istanbul, Turkey, for Dylan's sixtieth birthday celebration rather than organize the bash. In March 2001, I was offered an
all-expense-paid trip to play at a Bob Dylan birthday tribute at a Turk-
ish horse farm. I nearly accepted, but giving the matter some further
thought I came to the conclusion that I'd rather pay tribute to my fellow
Iron Ranger in Minneapolis. So I called Kevin Odegard and asked him
if it would be possible to get the *Blood on the Tracks* band back together
for one set. After a brief performing trip to New York City and a visit to
the Woody Guthrie Archives, I returned to Minneapolis and found that

Kevin had received affirmative replies from every band member except Bill Berg, who was still in Los Angeles.

It would be the first time the rest of the band—Billy Peterson, Gregg Inhofer, Peter Ostroushko, Chris Weber, and Kevin—had performed together since the 1974 sessions. They gathered in the Webers' basement in Minnetonka to rehearse their part of the show. "I had been out of contact with Chris for years," Odegard said. "When we got back together, he was the life of the party. He always had a wicked smile on his face like he was planning something devious. I was looking forward to seeing him every day, planning the set and writing the charts. He was a masterful guitar player. It was no accident that he turned out to be the de facto band leader for *Blood on the Tracks*."

"It was the first time I'd seen any of those guys for a long time," Peterson said. "I knew the KO Band; Kevin was working all the time, but I never played with those guys. It was a riot. We got together and did some songs. When I can see Inhofer—we were of the same cloth, a little more of a jazzier, progressive dude than some of the other guys. Kevin and those guys were not into jazz at all. We were in different camps, but I'm convinced the synergy was great: everybody was into it."

"How long had it been?" Inhofer mused. "Billy, I see here and there. I see Kevin occasionally. I didn't see Chris very often, because he wasn't really a [working] musician per se."

"The idea to reunite the studio band was good," Odegard said. "Although the roster was outrageously overbooked, [Metsa] pulled it off magnificently."

Other participants included G. B. Leighton, Curtiss A, Chris Osgood and Dave Ahl, Rank Strangers, Dave Morton, the Wicked Messengers, Mechanical Bull, December's Architects, Quick Grits, Robin Kyle, the Glenrustles, Sherwin Linton, the Front Porch Swingin' Liquor Pigs, Janie Miller, the Ranchtones, the Middle Spunk Creek Boys, Anne Deming, Strangecloud, Viovoom, Tom McDonald, Captain Blasted, the KO Band, Baby Grant Johnson, Kevin Bowe, Tim Gadban, Simba, Laurie Lindeen, Michael McElrath, Dan Rumsey, Medication, the Minor Planets, and Gene LaFond.

The bash started at 8 p.m. with Hugh Brown, one of Dylan's first roommates in Dinkytown, reading Dylan's "Last Thoughts on Woody Guthrie." I read a welcoming message from LeRoy Hoikkala, the drummer from Dylan's high school band, the Golden Chords. Then a parade of singers and musicians took the stage, performing cover versions from all eras of the Bob Dylan songbook. The scene backstage was like a hipsters' prom. Paul Cebar, the rhythm and blues master from Milwaukee, told the crowd, "Dylan, he ruined us all."

I introduced the *Blood on the Tracks* band at 11 p.m. They began with the song that kicked off the Minneapolis sessions, "Idiot Wind." To me, it was like watching five prizefighters going for a knockout in the first round. They romped through the rest of the album, delighting the swaying, shaking crowd of one thousand Dylan fans. At midnight, I joined the band for a version of "My Back Pages" with most of the crowd joining in on the familiar chorus: "I was so much older then, I'm younger than that now."

After six hours, forty acts, and more than seventy songs, the show came to a close with the entire building singing "I Shall Be Released," the hymn Dylan wrote during his seclusion in Woodstock with The Band in 1967. And as joyous as the long evening was, it almost rose to another level. One of Dylan's oldest friends, Larry Kegan, was among the celebrants; midway through the evening he called Dylan, who happened to be spending time at his Minnesota farm, and told him he should come to First Avenue for the show. Not so preposterous an idea: it had almost happened the previous year during the KO Band's reunion at Mayslack's. "We heard later from other parties that Bob had almost come down, as he had to Mayslack's," Odegard said. "*Almost* was the word—I was on the phone with David [Zimmerman], giving him directions. The next year when Bob was in town, he had the directions, and they were seriously considering it, but the rain did put a damper on it."

Three years later, the *Blood on the Tracks* band reunited again, this time complete with Bill Berg. He and his wife had retired from the Disney studios and moved from Los Angeles to North Carolina. On March 3, 2004, the band sold out the thousand-seat Pantages Theatre in downtown Minneapolis for a show called *Blood on the Tracks* Live. The poster advertising the event featured a sketch of Dylan and some of the other

Poster from the *Blood on the Tracks* reunion show in 2004. Courtesy of Kevin Odegard.

participants at Sound 80, made by the band's most famous illustrator. "The Dylan sketches—they came as an afterthought," said Berg. "They've been posters and T-shirts. Kevin Odegard approached me about doing a book, and they needed some sort of a visual reference to the sessions. What was in my memory? That's what prompted that. I did those over a weekend. I think we probably had a pretty busy week at Disney."

I played an opening set, and then the album was performed end to end by the Minneapolis Six, who were joined by Eric Weissberg, thus bringing together participants of both the Minnesota and New York *Blood on the Tracks* sessions for the first time. "It was good to have Eric Weissberg there," Berg said. "He could bring the New York sound. It was good to meet him. He was a very nice man. When Eric showed up, I think he thought he was going to play down to us, even though he was impressed with what we did on the record. He went on and on about how good the players were in Minneapolis. When we first started to rehearse for the 2004 concert, 'Tangled Up in Blue' and 'Idiot Wind,' it was almost tearful," Berg said. "All those years had gone by. Everybody was alive. I called my wife that afternoon and said, 'Oh, this feels so good to do this.' It was not just a rehash. It was one of the nicest musical experiences, especially with Gregg, and Billy Peterson, one of my absolute favorite bass players in the world. And Peter and Kevin and Chris—we were there because we loved doing this."

Once again, the musicians rehearsed at the Webers' house. "It took two or three rehearsals," Berg said. "I recall it was a smoky room. Two or three of the guys were pretty heavy smokers. It was like, 'I love this, but would you guys take it outside?'"

"It was all wonderful," Vanessa Weber said. "Eric Weissberg was there. They rehearsed in the basement. They all had a ball. We became good friends with Eric, who's just a delightful person. Those rehearsals were fun. I'd sometimes bake them cookies."

"Eric Weissberg was a guy who was always all-in on everything," Odegard said. "He was a big hit."

Inhofer had been waiting a long time to talk to Weissberg. "Eric, there's a question I've been wanting to ask you for twenty, thirty years," Inhofer said prior to the show.

"Well, why didn't you call me?" Weissberg replied.

"I didn't have your number!" Inhofer said. "Did you get performance royalties for *Blood on the Tracks*?"

"Yes. For nine months."

"Did you get a gold record?"

"I got a gold record for *Blood on the Tracks* and a gold single for 'Tangled Up in Blue.'"

"We never got any of that," Inhofer said. He found it particularly unjust because Weissberg didn't play a note on "Tangled Up in Blue."

When the band walked onto the Pantages stage, Berg found the enthusiastic welcome from the crowd deeply gratifying. "It was so warm," Berg said. "Some of us hadn't been in town for a long time. There was overwhelming support from the community. We did sort of a ragtag video—a real afterthought in those days, especially consumer video—but there we were."

In addition to playing a version of his own hit "Dueling Banjos" with Peter Ostroushko, Weissberg sang "You're Gonna Make Me Lonesome When You Go." There were several other guest vocalists that night, including Mary Lee Kortes, who sang "You're a Big Girl Now" and "Buckets of Rain"; Adam Levy, who sang "Idiot Wind"; Pat Hayes, who sang "Meet Me in the Morning"; Sherwin Linton, who sang "Shelter from the Storm"; and Martin Devaney, who sang "Lily, Rosemary and the Jack of Hearts," with comic cue-card assistance from Marc Percansky.

Of the Minneapolis band members, Inhofer sang "Tangled Up in Blue," Weber sang "If You See Her, Say Hello," and Odegard sang "A Simple Twist of Fate." It was a profoundly emotional night for Odegard, who had just coauthored a book called *A Simple Twist of Fate*, about the experience of making *Blood on the Tracks*. He was also battling substance abuse, and his marriage was falling apart: "Life was imitating art for me." Odegard continued:

I was performing Dylan's great breakup album—the divorce album—going through a divorce myself. I wasn't in the greatest shape in the world. It was emotional. It was cathartic. It was difficult, but charging through that great poetry in "Idiot Wind," "Tangled Up in Blue," and the rest of the songs together was therapy. I believe that I wasn't the only one feeling emotional about "Tangled Up in Blue." We'd all seen a lot of water under the bridge in the past thirty-five years, and it was a wonderful thing to get together. Fortunately, our friendships remained intact. We stayed in touch, all six of us.

Yet it was during his spotlight song that night that Odegard found he almost couldn't continue. "Anyone who survives substance abuse can tell you about their 'bottom,' the lowest moment in their life," Odegard said. "Bob Dylan had his; so did I. My bottom happened onstage on March 3, 2004, at the Pantages Theatre in Minneapolis. I was midway through my chosen song, 'A Simple Twist of Fate,' struggling to get through the fourth verse":

He woke up; the room was bare. He didn't see her anywhere.
He told himself he didn't care, pushed the window open wide;
Felt an emptiness inside to which he just could not relate,
Brought on by a simple twist of fate.

"At precisely the line 'He didn't see her anywhere,' I glanced out at the audience and caught sight of my then-wife, Mindy, in the second row." He continued:

My throat closed up and tears came forth like a spring gully washer, raining down on the stage. I swung around to face the band and finished the verse by tele-transporting the whole scene to waterfront Marseilles, then signaled for Martin Devaney to take a harmonica solo, collecting myself enough to get through two more verses. And there it was: the one person I had hurt the most was watching me melt down in public at what should have been a fine moment. I had a book out that very night, a sellout crowd in front of me, and a promise crystallizing for this ragtag brotherhood of uncredited musicians. I was never more alone in my life, before or since. The losses had mounted along with the wins, all of which felt empty and meaningless.

I've heard many people describe this same moment in their lives. Some found sobriety, some found Jesus, others found redemption and forgiveness. As I turned around to face the audience again, I felt a resolve pulsing through me like never before. Anger, self-pity, and remorse gave way to focus and determination as I regained the strength to finish the song. I no longer felt the cocktail straitjacket of benzodiazepines modulating my actions. By the last line and a flourishing strum of the final, haunting, low D chord, my mini-epiphany was complete. I have never doubted myself, as God made me, from that moment on.

The process of writing his book had been the final straw that broke the marriage, Odegard said. "While I was writing that book, the marriage was fish or cut bait, and I absented myself," he said. "I was locked in a room writing about those six minutes. Life imitated art: I ended up with a decent book and a broken marriage. Mindy and I were divorced in 2004. At the very time the book came out, I'd lost everything—home, car, marriage."

Soon after the Pantages concert, a friend dropped Odegard off at the Hazelden drug and alcohol treatment facility in Center City, Minnesota. He was assigned to a high-risk recovery unit ("the hard-case unit") and stayed there for four months. "It was a miserable experience—I wouldn't recommend it to anyone," Odegard said. "I did learn some valuable lessons, though, that carried through life. In the end I made a one-step program out of it. I made the decision to try something different. Bags of fan mail [for the book] came to Hazelden. I was really in the dumps. One inquisitive musician, Jeff Hill, arrived the day my divorce papers showed up. He was interested in getting to the bottom of the rumor that I had not played on *Blood on the Tracks*. He had heard me play many times and was obviously unimpressed." Nevertheless, Odegard and Hill became friends and eventually wrote a song together for Knut

Koupee, a Minneapolis guitar store. Sadly, Hill eventually died of throat cancer—a frequent cause of death among musicians.

Odegard had flirted with his own mortality, but during his long stay at Hazelden he began the process of restoring his health. "I made the best of it," he said. "I ran, got in shape, lost a lot of weight, and listened to a lot of Bruce Hornsby. I knew Bruce; I met him at the Roxy [in LA] when he was doing a showcase for ex-Zombie Paul Atkinson. I felt a kinship there. Bruce got me better, got me well. There was a five-mile run—I could circle the campus. I always had a digital cassette player. I know every word, every lick of Bruce Hornsby's albums. As much as anybody else, he kept me going."

"There was a couple of times he was so low I knew I couldn't really help him," said Nancy Bundt, who remained in contact with Odegard and continues to be a friend to this day:

> I'm certainly glad that he healed. It was hard for him that he had to go through that. Music helped—always. He began working with disadvantaged men. He started helping other people, and that really helped him. That changed him—a lot. He helped people who needed even more help than he needed. He's kind of a deep guy. It doesn't show that much, but when he needs to stand up and use it, it's there. A lot of times it was covered to other people, but I knew. When I first knew him—I don't think he'd want to be described this way—but he's kind of a creative genius. He has so many places of creativity in his head, and all the alcoholism just got in the way. Just blocked all that. Now in this phase of his life, he has access to it. He's an incredible writer, the way he uses words. The music was always good. The way he networked with people—he was always really interested. But he could piss people off right and left; he was good at that, too. I don't think he does that anymore. If he doesn't want to play with you, he doesn't play with you. He grew up.

The *Blood on the Tracks* reunions continued in 2005 when the studio band was inducted into the Minnesota Rock/Country Hall of Fame

The *Blood on the Tracks* Studio Band inducted into the Minnesota Rock/Country Hall of Fame on May 7, 2005 *(left to right)*: Stanley Kipper, Bill Berg, Gregg Inhofer, Kevin Odegard, Peter Ostroushko, Chris Weber. Courtesy of Kevin Odegard.

(now the Mid-America Music Hall of Fame). In May 2006, *Blood on the Tracks* Live played a gig at the storied Hibbing High School auditorium as part of the town's annual Dylan Days. Odegard, Peterson, Berg, Inhofer, and Ostroushko were there, along with Odegard's longtime drummer Stan Kipper. There was also a performance at University of Minnesota–Duluth and a museum opening in Minneapolis, with Paul Martinson in attendance. "We did all Bob tunes," Berg said. "For the Hibbing concert, we had to expand the repertoire."

In 2009, Odegard got the inspiration to put on an annual Dylan tribute. He was living in a sober house in St. Louis Park, riding his bicycle back and forth to work each day. One evening he happened to catch the sound of live music floating in the air while he was walking by the Wolfe Park amphitheater. "It was Greg Anderson, the piano player on my first album, playing piano," Odegard said. "Such a beautiful setting, a park surrounded by greenery. I thought, 'What a waste. We could make this so much better.' I looked around and visualized the park filled with happy families." That summer he and Stan Kipper reunited the KO Band and invited Peterson, Inhofer, and Ostroushko to do another *Blood on the Tracks* Live show. It was a smash, drawing a crowd of five thousand to the amphitheater, free of charge. The Dylan sidemen were joined by Chico Perez, Larry Suess, Scott Dercks, Kevin Bowe, Dan Israel, and Matt "Dr." Fink from Prince and the Revolution.

"My fortunes improved," Odegard said. "By September 2009, I was married to Susan Casey, living the happy life I thought I'd lost forever. Susan's a warm person. Her hospitality brought the old musical friend back into my life. I was my old, old friend again, the nineteen-year-old at the University of Minnesota with Stan Kipper."

At the 2010 St. Louis Park show, the *Blood on the Tracks* Live band highlighted songs from Dylan's *Blonde on Blonde* album. The core band included Peterson, Ostroushko, and Odegard, along with Kipper, Perez, Fink, Metsa, Israel, Dercks, Bowe, Gary Lopac, Lonnie Knight, Scott Sansby, Jeff Dayton, Billy Hallquist, Peter Lang, Alison Scott, Patty Peterson, Gretchen Seichrist, Adam Levy, Bobby Z, and Jim Steinworth.

Now living in North Carolina, Bill Berg did not return to the Twin Cities for what became annual tribute concerts at Wolfe Park. Nor did Weber, who had moved to California with his family. After the 2010 show, Inhofer decided not to participate in further St. Louis Park tributes. "There were about twelve or fourteen people onstage," Inhofer said. "I sang two songs off of *Blood on the Tracks*, and after the show my friend came up and said, 'Do you know you didn't get introduced after either song that you sang? Matt Fink and Bobby Z got introduced twice. You didn't get introduced once. No mention.' So I thought, 'Well, hell, I guess I don't have to do this anymore.' I never did another one when they asked. I said, 'Nah, no thanks.'"

Odegard made sure to keep Ostroushko in the fold, despite the fact that he'd become the most famous and in-demand member of the *Blood on the Tracks* Live band. "People around [Ostroushko] never liked me," Odegard said. "I never got close to his friends; I was never invited to birthday parties. But I had to have Peter on the St. Louis Park shows. Peter and I rode up to Hibbing and Duluth together, because I had my license removed by the Hennepin County sheriff at that point. We talked about alcohol, music, and other things. We were friends. We became closer personal friends than musical friends. Peter responded by charging an arm and a leg to perform with me. I had to put up with it, because I couldn't play a show without Peter sitting there."

In 2011, the band recorded a live version of Odegard's composition "The El Niño Suite" at Wolfe Park. "Peter takes lead on every song," Odegard said. "He'd never heard any of them before. They were complicated chord changes. I had trouble playing them, and I'd written them. He'd lead in with a figure from Bartók. His solos were described by himself as 'conversations with God.' He never fussed, never asked for anything, never made any requests, and his version of 'Girl from the North Country' always brought the house down. He had the best version. I included him at all the St. Louis Park shows."

Odegard treated the other musicians with equal respect: "I paid every musician a generous wage for every performance, recording and rehearsal in my entire career. Any musician who's ever played with me, and that's over a hundred, will tell you the same thing: they were paid and paid well. If we recorded a performance in St. Louis Park, they got the same pay for doing it in the studio. I was paying double or triple." He credits his mother—"Barbara Perkins Odegard, the angel in my life"—for making sure he could afford to pay his fellow musicians a fair wage. Sometimes, if needed, she would slip a $500 check into his bank account. The lesson was learned.

"I never did a free gig," Odegard said. "I respected and revered working musicians who have a very tough occupation that I was never brave enough to attempt. I paid Peter more because that's what he asked. Peter Ostroushko, in his lifetime, was arguably the best mandolin player on planet earth. How do you argue with that? You sell a guitar if you have to. I trusted him. He contributed much more than his share in every situation. If I paid him more, he was worth twice that."

In 2011, a second show was added at the Town Green in Maple Grove. The band continued to feature songs from *Blood on the Tracks*, but the three-hour shows included songs from many Dylan albums and eras. The featured performer in 2011 was Minnesota native Joyce Everson (born Joyce Everson Turnpenny) who had worked with Gordon

Lightfoot, Peter Frampton, and Jackson Browne. Many of the performers from past shows were back again.

The following year, the band again did two free shows, one in Maple Grove and one in St. Louis Park. Odegard was joined by his usual pals, including Kipper and Bobby Z, plus new guests the Daisy Dillman Band and Mary Jane Alm. It was the final year for Odegard, who turned the annual gatherings over to Billy Hallquist. In 2013, the event was renamed *Salute to the Music of Bob Dylan.*

———————

Odegard's interest in *Blood on the Tracks* had not waned, but his predominant interest now was advocating for the Minneapolis musicians to receive their long-overdue credit. Dylan had embarked on a career-spanning series of *Bootleg* albums, featuring outtakes and alternate versions of songs from all phases of his career. The motivation was to finally capture some of the profits from his heavily bootlegged catalogue, and to preserve copyrights to performances not previously issued. But there was no particular pattern to the reissues, and given Dylan's legendary privacy, it was anyone's guess what the next bootleg volume would include. As each was released, however, Odegard's hopes for a *Blood on the Tracks* box set increased. The so-called New York sessions bootleg from 1974 had been circulating for years. If Columbia would officially release all the studio takes from the album, the Minnesota Six would finally get their names included in the package.

Odegard heard the acetate bootleg from the New York sessions, and he was a fan: "There is a version of 'Idiot Wind' with Paul Griffin, my personal hero. Paul Griffin plays the opening piano on 'American Pie.' He plays on so many hit records I can't name them all. He came in and overdubbed this very scary, dark organ Hammond B3 in New York. It's as good—and many people say better—than the great version we cut in Minneapolis."

Odegard suspected there were a few outtakes of the Minneapolis sessions that could be released in a box set. He had looked for them, but nothing had turned up. He was not defensive about those who compared the New York versions of the songs to the Minneapolis versions:

> The New York sessions were wonderful. I think that they would have stood on their own and been another great volume in Bob Dylan's canon. When he came home for the holidays in 1974, in discussions with his brother David Zimmerman, they felt there was an opportunity. And David may or may not have pointed out to him that none of these songs would go on the radio. It was not the current format; it wouldn't fit into AOR [album-oriented radio] and whatever the Abrams people were programming in those days. So he convinced Bob to try one song, and that turned into five, and they replaced the New York versions. Not everybody was happy about that, but that's the way it played out, and the record is still, as we sit here today, his best-selling studio album of all time. That speaks volumes to those who [prefer] this series of sessions or that series of sessions.

Odegard's hopes were realized on November 2, 2018, when Columbia released *More Blood, More Tracks: The Bootleg Series, Volume 14*, a six-CD boxed set including every known take recorded for *Blood on the Tracks*. Alas, there were no outtakes found from the Minneapolis sessions. Most of the set consists of Dylan's multiple attempts to find the right way to present his songs in New York's A&R Studio. The five takes from Sound 80 that ended up on the album were remastered and remixed, however, and the individual instruments sound more distinct than they did on the original album. For the New York tracks, some postproduction effects were minimized. As Odegard recalled:

> For *More Blood, More Tracks*, [reissue engineer] Steve Addabbo de-Ramoned the New York stuff. He took all the echo out and took the mastering effects off the Minnesota stuff. It's not quite as jangly, but rich, pure, and acoustic. Technology has improved a lot since then. Steve underproduced it, not overproduced it. I like the new recordings much better. I can listen to all six discs in a row and

not get tired. You can hear the genesis of each song. It's interesting to me to see that. Dylan originally wrote every song in [open] E. In the Minneapolis sessions he's in standard tuning and didn't use capos. Bob was at the peak of his musician powers at that time. Bob was on his game. You hear things about him—"He plays out of tune." People don't like his singing, but I'll tell you, at those sessions he knew what he wanted, and if he didn't get it from us, he did it himself. That's him on the B3 organ: in the studio it sounded a lot like *Highway 61 Revisited*.

Even better than hearing the recordings in a new way was that the musicians finally could see their names—spelled correctly—credited to the tracks they played on. "It was the greatest story of most of our lives," Odegard said. "It culminated the campaign that took forty-five years. Metsa started it in 2001 at the Depot downtown [First Avenue]. In 2004, it was the Pantages. The past twenty years have been dedicated to getting our names printed on something. For most of us, it was a watershed moment and an emotional high. November 2, 2018, was the culmination for all of it. For everybody."

Odegard gathered in a television studio with Inhofer, Peterson, and Ostroushko to listen to and talk about the box set. "It floored me," Odegard said, then looked around at his fellow musicians. "And I think it affected you, too. Because by the time we were done listening to 'Tangled Up in Blue,' we were all in tears, and so were the two cameramen, and they are he-men who cover Vikings games. It was a very emotional experience to hear this."

"Yeah, it is," Peterson agreed.

"I'm welling up now," Odegard said.

"When *More Blood* came out, it really cleared up a lot of stuff," Peterson said later. "They did a phenomenal job. I was really impressed. Everybody in the industry is impressed with those remixes."

Berg had been alerted by Odegard that the box set was about to be released, and he was sent a copy by Dylan's management office. He gave a close listen to the New York versions of the songs and was satisfied that time had validated the contributions he and the other Minnesotans had made. He even admitted he would like to have played on more than just half the songs. "There was one," Berg said. "Richard Crooks did 'Meet Me in the Morning,' and maybe another—those I definitely would have liked to play on. But two different drummers added to the diversity of the sound of the record. That was the personality at that moment. Like it or not, that's what they did. I thought [the New York session] was a little out of tune in places, maybe—it had a personality that seemed a little not committed enough for the more intense stuff that he was writing."

Berg has never attempted to claim credit for the success of the album, however. "As private a guy as Bob is—I haven't talked to him one time since we did the record—he's the core of this," Berg said of his fellow Hibbing expat. "He did the writing. Maybe not enough credit is given to him, rather than us trying to seek our credit. Maybe David Zimmerman has not gotten enough credit, with Kevin, for bringing the right people together. It was totally flattering to me to be in a Bob session. Maybe Billy would say the same thing. They put together a rhythm section that would stand up to Bob's music and play it the way we felt it needed to be played."

Berg continued: "A couple of years ago I read *Restless Daughter* about Joni Mitchell. Joni really enjoyed the New York recordings. I stopped reading the book right then. As much as I love Joni Mitchell, if you're that critical of what we did naturally. . . . We had no preconceptions, we just played from our hearts. If you want to look at the New York sessions, they sound dated, folky. They have their own personality, but at same time I think we gave Bob's music a little bit of grit and power that was not happening in New York. I still think some of the stuff— 'Buckets of Rain'—had a nice funkiness to it. The difference between the New York and Minneapolis bands created something unique. The whole project worked."

When *More Blood, More Tracks* was issued in 2018, Chris Weber could finally see, in black and white, his name listed in the credits. On page 56 of the accompanying booklet, under the five songs recorded at

Sound 80 on December 27 and 30, 1974, the credits read: "Bob Dylan: vocals, guitar, harmonica, organ, mandolin. Chris Weber: guitar." "It meant a lot to him, but it didn't do anything for him," Vanessa said. "People weren't calling him up, except our kids. It was kind of tardy. But he was very pleased. He did get the platinum record three years ago. Kevin told him how to apply for them, to prove you were on it. Then you have to buy it. It was about $350."

After the release of the six-CD set, there were still those who insisted that the New York versions of the songs were superior to the Minneapolis versions. Inhofer's verdict: "Everybody's got an asshole, like opinions," he said. "That record brought Dylan back to AM radio. I don't think the original tracks would have. 'Tangled Up in Blue' brought him back to AM radio as a force, and everything he put out after that was a force."

Inhofer was glad to finally receive credit for his work on the album, but to his mind it didn't eliminate decades of injustice. "I wasn't ever bitter,'" he said. "I was pragmatic, as was Peter [Ostroushko]. He and I saw eye to eye. I didn't hold [Dylan] up here like he walked on water, and a lot of people did and do. I was not one of them, and neither was Peter. To be perfectly honest, we got screwed. The six Minneapolis musicians got screwed. I'm not claiming anything other than synchronicity. We were synchronistically brought together, and it worked. It worked so well that his album still keeps on regenerating itself over the years."

So much so that Inhofer can count on periodic reminders of the album's continuing success nearly five decades later:

In the late '80s or early '90s, I'm sitting at my coffee table with a stack of bills that I can't pay, watching MTV. . . . They're doing the top 100 rock albums of all time. "Number 25, Bob Dylan's *Blood on the Tracks!*" They're playing "Tangled Up in Blue." I'm listening to myself and I'm looking at this stack of bills and say, "Ah, this is the definition of irony. That's what it is. I get it now." Another time, my stepson was playing *Rock Band,* and he opened up the secret song: "Early one morning the sun was shining, I was laying in bed." I'm going, "Holy shit . . ."

The box set *More Blood, More Tracks* has added more money to the Dylan coffers, but not much for Inhofer and the other Minneapolis players. "We never got performance royalties," Inhofer said. "I have thought many times over the past ten, twenty years that I should sue Sony, because they bought Columbia and they buy any baggage. All I want is performance royalties that I should have gotten—plus interest since 1975. I have no idea what that would be. I was naive. I was twenty-four years old. I'll take 50 percent of the responsibility." He said he can't imagine any contemporary superstar allowing his studio musicians to go uncredited and, essentially, unpaid. "I should have gone to David when that second pressing came out, but I didn't even know or care when it came out the first time. I was listening to McLaughlin and Return to Forever and Weather Report."

If there wasn't any extra money coming back to the Minneapolis Six when the box set was released, at least they would all live to see their names permanently linked with one of rock's all-time great records. "I'm glad that *More Blood, More Tracks* came out before people started passing away," Odegard said. "I wish Paul Martinson was here to see that. He was very proud of that work. He was equal to any musician on that session." Sadly, Martinson has been joined in the great musical beyond by two more participants in the Sound 80 sessions.

Epilogue

"WHAT THEY DO WITH THEIR LIVES"

CHRIS AND VANESSA WEBER RETIRED FROM THE REAL ESTATE business in 2008, during one of America's most significant recessions. "Everything had tanked," Vanessa said. "Our home wasn't worth what we thought it was, so we came out to California. We had two grandchildren by that time. We moved into the Sierra Mountains in Placerville, halfway to Tahoe, and spent a wonderful year of doing nothing, living on our savings. Then after that, we went down to Los Angeles to check out what [Chris] could do there, but it wasn't comfortable for a troubadour. A single person with a guitar was not what people were listening to."

The Webers spent a year setting up their son's marijuana dispensary in Los Angeles, making use of Vanessa's office skills and Chris's marketing instincts to get the business running. Then they moved north to Concord, a community in the San Francisco Bay Area, to be closer to their daughter and her three children. Chris recorded with other musicians, and both found work, Vanessa as a substitute teacher and Chris repairing guitars. In an odd twist of fate, Weber was hired by the company that helped run him out of business when he owned the Podium in Minneapolis—Guitar Center. "It was a blow, but we were tired of real estate," Vanessa said.

Weber once again relied on his experience and creativity to propose a center dedicated to guitar repair. A month later he received a letter from Guitar Center's corporate office informing him that they'd already thought about establishing a repair center. "Then they did everything we said, except put Chris in charge of it," Vanessa said. "He worked there about a year. He was so good at repairing them they had to take in another person."

Weber once again advocated for the setup idea that had made the Podium so successful with beginning guitar students. Guitar Center liked that idea, too, and allowed Chris to run the operation from his home. He soon quit Guitar Center and opened up his own shop. "It was constant," Vanessa said. "It was old farts like us who knew quality and had their guitars for a long time who trusted him to fix their $5,000 guitar. He taught himself electric guitars. He was quite in demand. I still get calls for him."

Their son left the marijuana dispensary in Los Angeles and moved to Concord because his girlfriend had a baby. "He had his child every other week," said Vanessa. "He'd drive up, pick him up, bring him here. It was great because we'd have all our grandchildren in one place. It was right around that time Chris opened his own shop in 2017."

Then Chris became ill with COPD.

The Webers stayed in touch with Minnesotans, especially Morrie Lazarus, Chris's closest friend. They rarely returned to the state because of Vanessa's teaching job and their responsibilities as grandparents. Chris Weber eventually succumbed to COPD on January 27, 2021. He was seventy-three. "At his funeral, we had a lot of his friends there," Vanessa said. "We assumed we'd have a very small funeral, but there were over one hundred, even with Covid."

"He was a soulful player, not just good at playing fast notes," Kevin Odegard said. "He really drew you in. He was magnetic and charismatic and had a wonderful singing voice. He was a genuinely kind and generous human being. I miss him every day."

———

Peter Ostroushko suffered a serious stroke in January 2018 that rendered his left arm useless and made it impossible for him to play any of the instruments on which he was so proficient, including the bouzouki that was given to him by Kevin Odegard and his wife, Susan. "We were familiar with the instrument, so one year on his birthday we gifted him the bouzouki," Odegard said. "It was not associated with a gig, but just because we loved Peter. That's the kind of guy he was."

In July 2018, an overflow crowd attended a potluck fundraiser for Ostroushko and his wife, Marge, at St. Joan of Arc Catholic Church in South Minneapolis. Though seated in a wheelchair, Ostroushko found the strength and determination to speak for twenty minutes. "I can't play an instrument," he was quoted by music writer Jon Bream in the *Star Tribune*. "My voice is compromised from the stroke." At that point, he was interrupted by the ringing of church bells. "Hello?" Ostroushko said, to much laughter.

He told stories from his long and colorful musical past, thanked his wife and daughter, his fellow musicians, and tried to assure the audience that he intended to play again someday. "I want to dispel a myth," he said. "I got a phone call from someone who left a message on the phone that they wouldn't be making it to my last concert. . . . This can't possibly be my last concert." The void was partially filled that night by many of Ostroushko's longtime musical collaborators, including Becky Reimer Thompson, Dakota Dave Hull, Laura MacKenzie, Ann Reed, and Ukrainian singer Natalie Nowytski. The benefit raised almost $90,000 for Ostroushko's medical expenses.

Bill Berg, who hadn't seen Ostroushko between the second night at Sound 80 and the 2004 show at the Pantages, had only recently had the time to listen to all the music Ostroushko recorded. "I had no idea how many records he had done," Berg said. "The great amount of diversity and styles knocked me out. My wife probably heard him more on *Prairie Home Companion* than I did, even though I knew he was on the show. I wasn't a regular listener to Garrison, but I loved his show when I heard it on Saturday nights on the way to a gig."

After the stroke, Ostroushko recorded ten episodes of a podcast he called *My Life and Time as a Radio Musician*. Each episode is set up by stories from Ostroushko's past and includes a number of performances, mostly from *Prairie Home Companion*, with various musicians, recorded between 1974 and 1980. Becky Thompson got a call from Ostroushko when he was putting together his podcasts. "I have to get permission from everybody to use them on my podcast," Ostroushko told her. "I'm calling you because many of the first ten years, you and I played together."

"I know, and you never hired me for any of your big concerts, Peter," Thompson said in mock petulance.

"Out of sight, out of mind," he joked.

Thompson visited Ostroushko often when he was undergoing rehab. "We'd just chat," Thompson said.

He was in pretty rough shape. He did all of the podcasts after the stroke. He got a hard drive with forty years of all his performances on *Prairie Home.* He meticulously went through all of them. I was over at the apartment one night, and he goes, "You've got to listen to this." He played my version of "Woodstock," and I said, "Oh my gosh, where did you get that?" He told me what he was doing. That was pretty exciting. I wish he could have . . . well, we all wish he could have done more. I love just listening to his narratives. He made them very visual: walking down Cedar Avenue, going to the Riverside Café, going to the Extemp. Amazing how many people were on that.

"We drifted apart for many years," said his former five-string banjo partner Jim Tordoff, who no longer plays publicly because of a tremor that has developed in his right hand. Tordoff recalled:

Then he did a three-CD set [*Mando Chronicles,* Red House, 2012], which was sort of his magnum opus. We played on one of those tunes. That sort of brought us back together again. By this time, I was playing with a four-piece band called Ivory Bridge. We asked Peter to play fiddle for us on the CD we were making, then he was gigging with us. We'd be gigging off and on. Sometimes he couldn't make the gig. My last gig was at the Bakken Museum on the west side of Lake Calhoun. Before that, we played some gig somewhere— you lose track after you play a couple of hundred spots. We played monthly in our last couple of years of being together at Dulono's

Pizza, a longtime string-band bluegrass venue. My musicianship with Peter basically bookended his and my musical careers. We started out and ended up together. It was a joy to get back together and play music with him again. I feel very privileged that I was able to do that.

"We all felt pretty devastated when he could no longer play," Thompson said. "The last few times I talked with him, I was saying that I wanted to do a new CD, and I was trying to figure out if I wanted old and new recordings. He was saying I should do a retrospective, get some of the old recordings. He said I could use some of these that he had on the podcast. I was going to drag him and help me listen. I still hear his voice saying, 'When are you going to start that project?'"

On his website, Ostroushko offered advice for aspiring musicians: "Dig up the yard and plant a garden. Vegetables, flowers, whatever gets your socks off. Getting your hands in the dirt will teach you all you need to know about being a musician. See it through—from the backbreaking work of tilling the soil, until the fruits of your labor show themselves at the end of the growing season. The planting of the seed till the plant produces its bounty is watching God at his creative best. What inspiration! Plus, if you can't get any gigs, you won't starve."

Ostroushko died of heart failure on February 24, 2021, at the age of sixty-seven. Thompson, who still plays occasionally (her thirteen-year-old granddaughter now joins her on the fiddle), was at the cemetery when Ostroushko's ashes were interred in August 2021. "That was pretty incredible," she said.

Dean Magraw and Rachel Frank played two songs during the ceremony. The last song was "Heartland." That song makes me cry anyway, but I just fell apart during that. Dean was crying, Rachel was crying, I mean everybody was crying, just knowing everything he'd accomplished. After he passed away, all these accolades came in. People were saying he did this and he did that. I was talking to his wife, Marge, one day, and I said, "I really feel terrible because I don't know half the stuff he did." Marge said, "I didn't either."

Some of the stuff that was coming in she said she had no recollection of any of it. He never said anything about himself or his accomplishments. It was all about the music, his family, and his friends. That was basically Peter: his family first, then music, and his friends right after. I felt very honored to be one of his friends. I wish I could go talk to him and make my chocolate chip cookies for him. I miss him—a great deal.

––––––––

After a lifetime as a professional musician, playing in a multitude of bands and mastering countless styles, Gregg Inhofer believes he has overcome what he describes as an inability to assert himself. He doesn't recall specifically when it happened, but one harrowing experience comes to mind. "It might have been 2005, when I left my second wife, because that one just about killed me," he said. "Every time I would drive home from a gig to Shakopee, there was this black cloud that would be heavier and heavier, and the weight on my shoulders would get heavier the closer I got. One night getting home from a gig at a casino in Wisconsin, coming up to Rock City, with white knuckles, I went, 'Yep, I could run right into the bridge, right into the piling, and it would all be over. Floor that truck, here it comes'—and at the last second, my two boys' faces flashed before me. I could not. But I just about quit music, living out there in Shakopee."

He gradually found his way back. He's not as active as he used to be—or would like to be—but he has a lot of music he'd still like to share with the public. He has carried around a batch of tapes from This Oneness/Brainiac for forty years that he's transferred to digital format and plans to release them. He was contacted by a music fan in Germany who offered to help him with European and Japanese distribution of what he hopes will be a three-CD issue of all three albums recorded by the band, the last two of which were never released.

Inhofer said there will be no reunion performances by This Oneness. "It would take me literally two months of five-days-a-week doing scales, of practice, just to get ready to rehearse, to learn the stuff again," he said. "Because, God, I listen to it and think, 'Wow.' But it holds up. All these years later, the stuff holds up."

Inhofer has released two CDs of his own music since the Dylan reunion shows started: *Inside*, a live recording made at Peace Lutheran Church in Coon Rapids in 2006; and 2011's *Music for the Upright Walking*, featuring such Twin Cities luminaries as Dale and Bob Strength, Eric Gravatt, bassist Charles Fletcher, and saxophonist Jason Parvey. Unfortunately, Gregg Inhofer and the Cockeyed Band found very few gigs.

"Since 2005, when I kind of reinvented myself, I can't find an agent to get me any work," he said. "Because I'm old? I don't know. I was in bands that worked five, six, seven nights a week. There's not that kind of work anymore. People don't go out to clubs as much. They'll go to little bars, but there's not that much live music anymore. Certainly not the clubs there used to be, where people would come dressed to the nines to go out. Hotels don't have bands like they used to. So you put on your own gigs. We did a few of those with the Cockeyed Band."

His work now tends to come as a supporting musician for other artists' songs. He plays in a Lovin' Spoonful tribute band called Spoonful of Love. The group got its start when original Spoonful drummer Joe Butler became the frontman of the group after the departure of songwriter and lead singer John Sebastian. "They hired Mike Arturi twenty-five years ago to play drums, but during Covid they weren't interested in going out," Inhofer said. "Mike wanted to play, so he put together a tribute band. We've been doing shows, live-streaming, theaters, and things like that. I play keyboards and guitar. I'm John Sebastian, doing fourteen out of eighteen songs. It's okay. It's not the most fun I've ever had, but it's okay."

He also backed the Blues Brothers (Dan Aykroyd and Jim Belushi) at Mystic Lake Casino in 2018 and at a corporate gig for a gaming company in which Aykroyd has a stake. "Jim was the driving force," Inhofer said. "All my communication came from his office in LA. He was the only one who showed up for soundcheck. Dan was nice enough, but he didn't want to do that much. We did the show, he did his shtick, I walked past his dressing room, and he said, 'Good job.' They don't work a lot. They carried an eight-piece band: drummer, bass, two guitars, three horns, and three singers, a guy and two women. They didn't carry a keyboard player. I knew the soundman; he said they made 150 grand for one night. There was fifty grand for expenses, and a hundred for Jim and Dan to split."

As has been the case throughout most of his professional life, Inhofer is once again a member of multiple bands. One is the Jerks of Fate, the backing band for Curtiss A [Almstead]. Curtiss A's own recording career goes back to the punk era of the late '70s, and every year since John Lennon's murder in 1980, he has organized and starred in a tribute concert for the slain Beatle at First Avenue. Inhofer has played keyboards in the annual Lennon show for many years, including 2020, when Covid-19 forced the show to be live-streamed with no audience. Inhofer is also in a band called the Dahlias, fronted by Curtiss A's girlfriend, Gini Dodds:

> I told her, "Gini, I don't want to play with you because you're Curt's girlfriend. I want to play with you because I love your material." It's just good stuff. Don't ever tell Curt this, but I swear to God, he moves around the stage like Bono, and he hates Bono. I love Curt Almstead, that's why I put up with Curtiss A. I told him that to his face, and he said, "Yep, they're two different people. I get it." His idea is that when he's onstage, he wants the band before him to wish they were never onstage, and the band after him to wish they didn't have to. That's his mentality. Then you see Curt Almstead at his house, and he's got an apron on, he's vacuuming, and he says, "Oh, the cookies are almost done." He makes a great chocolate chip cookie.

Inhofer played keyboards on Curtiss A's 2020 album *Jerks of Fate* and plays keyboards with the Dahlias, but he'd rather be playing a different instrument. "I hate keyboards now," he said. "They're just old. I like them okay, but I'd rather play guitar or bass. Because I never learned guitar. I never learned the fret board. I know where A is, I know where D is, but I play with shapes and patterns, like I always did. I never wanted to stray from that. I always wanted to be a rock guitar player, not any kind of jazz player. I do that on the keyboard."

Despite decades of misgivings about how the *Blood on the Tracks* band was treated, Inhofer continues to be followed by the Dylan connection. In spring 2021, he received a text from promoter Jeff Taube inviting him to play keyboards at a Bob Dylan eightieth birthday tribute show at First Avenue on May 24. "I'm pretending to text back, 'Why the FUCK would I want to celebrate Bob Dylan's birthday?'" Inhofer said. "My son looked at me and he goes, 'You should do it.' 'Yeah, you're right, I should.' I wrote him back and said, 'Yeah.' And I'm really glad I did."

The show took place before a crowd of just seventy-four people, due to Covid-19 restrictions, but it was live-streamed. The core band consisted of Inhofer on organ, Noah Levy on drums, Barb Brynstad on bass, Steve Brantseg on guitar, and Matt Fink on piano. A number of other guest artists, including Billy Peterson, took the stage at various points to play and sing Dylan songs of their choice. For Inhofer, preparing for and playing all those Dylan songs was a revelation. "Over the years, I heard all the popular Dylan stuff, but I don't think I listened to all the popular albums," Inhofer said. "I never bought the albums. I was listening to Frank Zappa and the Velvet Underground. So in learning about forty songs for this show, everybody had their own version. 'I want to do the 1978 version from Madison Square Garden of this song.'" He familiarized himself with the songs he didn't know by researching them on YouTube and was amazed to discover that for almost every song on his list, there were fifteen or twenty versions:

One song I learned from the record, then the person [in the tribute band] changed their mind and said they wanted to change the key and do a different version, a live version. Okay, no problem, so I charted it out and changed it to A. Listening to it, I'm going, "Wait a minute, the lyrics are the same, but the song is completely different—the arrangement is different, the whole feel is different, the chords are different." I got a new respect for Dylan that I didn't have. I've always respected him as a lyricist, as the voice of a generation, but as I've always said, harmonically speaking, it didn't do much for me. But that was in 1975. I was pretty naive at the time. I saw he's just constantly trying to reinvent for himself.

I got new respect for his voice in 2004 when we did the Pantages show. I learned "Tangled Up in Blue"—I'd never done it before. I'm learning it and I'm going, "Wow, I see what he wanted to do, I see where he was going with it." But he didn't give a shit. That wasn't his vehicle; singing was not his thing. It was just a way to get his words out. I think it became a little more important to him as I see all this live stuff, because, boy, he was kicking ass on some of those vocals, and I'd never heard that.

When Inhofer looks back over his own life and career—all the places he's played, all the bands he's been in, the lifestyle choices he made—he marvels that he's still around and still playing. "I've many times thought I should be dead," he said. "I must have a purpose. And I think the purpose is to be my granddaughter's grandfather." Viviana Isabella Inhofer is his life now. "I always say I'm not totally proud of my past, but I don't run from it. My mantra is, 'All roads lead to now.' I'm very happy, and I couldn't see it any other way."

Even though Bill Berg and his wife, Kaaren, had grandkids and many music industry friends in LA, the traffic, brush fires, and earthquakes they'd dealt with for nearly forty years had worn them down. They decided to leave Southern California. "We looked around, picked up one of those *Best 100 Places to Retire*, and discovered a nice niche in western North Carolina—the Asheville, Hendersonville, Waynesville area." They moved to North Carolina in 2004. Over the years, he returned to Minnesota for several of the *Blood on the Tracks* Live reunions but has settled into a new musical community where he works with several bands and does session work.

"Probably one of the nicest things happened in 2019," Berg said. "I got a call from a recording studio I work at called Echo Mountain. They asked me if I'd be interested in playing on the next Judy Collins record. Judy is now eighty-two and sounds so good still, in my estimation. Her road band is a bluegrass band called Chatham County Line. It's a mix of bluegrass and folk. On the record we did one of my favorite Joni

Mitchell tunes called 'River.' I never worked with Joni, but I did one of her songs with Judy Collins singing it."

During the recording, Collins's bass player approached Berg and told him he never worked with drummers. "I hope this will work," he said.

"We're going to make it work," Berg said, drawing on a lifetime of experience backing acoustic artists, including Bob Dylan. "We're going to listen to each other. You're a good player."

Berg plays in several house bands at clubs and craft breweries. He also plays with members of Steve Martin and Martin Short's touring band, the Steep Canyon Rangers. "I'm not in the band, but I play with some of the members," he said. "They won a Grammy a few years ago. I've been busy, aside from the pandemic and the fact that everybody was out of work—except virtually. I did a year and a half of pretty much nothing, but I'm back at it again. [The jobs] are coming along a little slower. It gives me a chance to pick and choose a little more rather than take whatever comes around. The musicianship is high enough around here that I feel challenged."

———————

In 2015, Billy Peterson had the pleasure of returning to his earliest days as a jazz bassist, producing the album *Pinnacle* for the Irv Williams Trio, the group that gave him his start way back in 1970. As a performer, Peterson released the jazz albums *Hope Street MN* in 2002 with Tony Hymas and Eric Gravatt; *I've Been Ringing You* with Bill Carrothers and Dave King in 2012; *Next Door* with Dave Hazeltine in 2016; and *Ricky Peterson and the Peterson Brothers* in 2021.

He lives in Bloomington, Minnesota, not far from the site of the old Metropolitan Stadium, where both his father and mother served as ballpark organists for the Minnesota Twins. Peterson also has a cabin in Whitefish, Montana. He has five children, ranging in age from fifty to thirty-one. "They're real good musicians," Peterson says. "My oldest daughter is a kinesiologist. My next is a United Health Care executive. My third daughter is a sweet hippie. My son Will is a singer and piano player, like Michael McDonald, and my son Rick plays bass, guitar, and piano. I do a lot of playing with my sons. It's real rewarding to go out and hang with my boys."

Peterson acknowledges that a lifetime in music is not the easiest way to keep a marriage intact. "I've been single since my divorce. I didn't get married to my second partner. My first two girls are from my first marriage. We all know what the music business is," he said. "You're not punching a clock. The perils of that are trying with the music business. Not being a young man full of testosterone helps."

When he's in the Twin Cities, he continues to play with old friends, including Gregg Inhofer, at Crooners Lounge and Supper Club in Northeast Minneapolis. He has a jazz trio that features piano, bass, and drums. "I tend to go for things with a high artistic level," Peterson said. "My heart and soul are really in the creative process, bringing the right musicians together, for great sound quality."

It's a family trait. Peterson's oldest sister, Linda, is seventy-five and still playing and singing. His sister Patty is ten years younger than Linda and also still active as a singer and jazz host on KBEM in Minneapolis. His brother Ricky is currently the keyboard player for Fleetwood Mac. "You can look up his stuff; he's done everything," Peterson said. "He was the first guy in town with a Minimoog synth. The first record I had him play on was a record with Bob Rockwell. He got a five-star review, and he was just fifteen at the time. He was Prince's producer at Paisley Park. He did 'The Most Beautiful Girl in the World,' a Prince song that was a Revlon commercial. Ricky got me hired to do some orchestrating for Prince, though I never played with him."

Paul Peterson, the youngest sibling, is a keyboard and bass player discovered in high school by Prince, who dubbed him St. Paul and put him in a band called The Family in 1985. He released his first solo album on MCA in 1987, a project that included Billy on bass, sister Patty on vocals, mother Jeanne on piano, and brother Ricky playing synth and coproducing the album. Three more solo albums followed, and he joined Billy in the Steve Miller Band for several years.

"We didn't call ourselves the First Family of Minnesota Music, but other people decided that," said Billy Peterson. "We always took pride in our family. Our family was very into the music scene, in the wake of our parents. We kind of got some grandfather clause because our name was Peterson, but to say we were driven by our name would not be correct. We were driven by passion to be the best we could. I've been very lucky, blessed, to always find something creative. Certain things become more important to you. I don't have to do anything for money anymore. I never did. Money kind of follows you around. I'm doing it for the passion of music. I'm still playing all the time. You pursue things—at my age, it's more important to know why am I here. You got five minutes left. That's what I'm gravitating to right now. A super-high level—it's just what I do. That's how I'm going down, swinging."

Kevin Odegard hasn't been in contact with David Zimmerman for fifteen years. "He's retired in Arizona," Odegard said. "He owns a golf course in Minnesota—Pheasant Acres, just north of New Hope. It's just down the road from his house, toward Maple Grove. The Dylan compound is down that road."

Odegard is retired as well. His last hurrah came in September 2018 at the Cavern Club in Liverpool, where the Beatles got their start in the early 1960s. He booked the appearance for himself and longtime musical partner Gary Lopac through Clark Gilmour, a regular performer at the Cavern Club and the band liaison for Liverpool's annual Beatleweek. "It was like going to the Temple of the Four Lads," he said. "That was the culmination of a lifetime interest. Gary and I got up and played 'Tangled Up in Blue' and 'Two of Us.' The crowd went wild. We got fan letters. People were wonderful. I couldn't live-stream it on Facebook because the signal didn't reach street level."

Odegard said conditions were stifling in the crowded underground music club. "It had to be 103 degrees onstage," he said. "I'm pretty sure Susan thought I was dead. In the few moments after we came offstage, I was all in. I couldn't move. I was on the floor of the Cavern Club. I'm pretty sure what was going through Susan's mind was, 'He died doing what he loved.' That was the pinnacle of my journey, the top of the mountain for me."

At the conclusion of their performance, Odegard and Lopac shook hands with Gilmour and repeated John Lennon's famous phrase about where the young Beatles were headed: "Toppermost of the Poppermost!" But in reality, that was the end of Odegard's performing career. He no longer plays guitar due to arthritis. He donated the Martin D-28 he played on "Tangled Up in Blue" to the Bob Dylan Center in Tulsa, Oklahoma, which opened to the public in May 2022. The center is home to a treasure trove of previously unreleased recordings, film performances, rare and unseen photographs, and handwritten lyric manuscripts— including the notebooks in which he wrote out the lyrics to the songs that made up *Blood on the Tracks*.

"I can't play chords anymore," Odegard said. "I bought a nice Hawaiian five-string. It sounds like a Rickenbacker but it's like a ukulele. Django Reinhardt had only three fingers—listen to him. He proved you can always play."

Odegard and his wife were last in Minnesota in 2018. They now live in Florida, where Odegard spent many hours at his grandparents' house as a boy, listening to the adults play the standards from the Great American Songbook while they drank martinis. His old friend Nancy Bundt visits each year. "I'm so happy for his life now," Bundt said. "I tell him and his wife all the time—'I'm happy for your happiness.' I really like her. I'm glad he's got her."

"There's a straight line in my life from beginning to now, a constant life-affirming interest in music," he said. "Now I'm collecting archives, getting some LA stuff, and working on a new album called *Everything's Cool*. The cover is a cigarette dangling from my mouth in Moscow in 1988. It's a collection of things that I think are good enough to re-record. I'm making some progress on a memoir and fiction called *Jump Start* about a geezer band—using Kickstarter. It's *Get Shorty* versus *Spinal Tap*. I have time now. I don't have a job to go to. I'm off the grid. Music keeps me insulated from the big, bad world out there. I'm unencumbered by the things of the material world."

The spiritual world is a different matter. Occupying a large part of that world for Odegard is the creative genius of Bob Dylan. "I used the song 'Idiot Wind' at a very difficult time in my life, without the music," Odegard said. "I can quote it from start to finish. It's a song about the real world. It's a song about recovering. That's a song about owning what is real about the world, and it is literature in its very truest form. The folks who were part of the literary community who objected to Bob's getting the Nobel [Prize for literature] maybe haven't spent enough time reading those lyrics."

But when it comes to Dylan songs, nothing will ever match "Tangled Up in Blue" for Odegard. He concurs with his daughter, who told him the six minutes of that song make up the defining moment of his musical career. "So my music career lasted six minutes," Odegard said. "I'm proud of those six minutes every time I step on an elevator or walk through a shopping center. I hear it at work. There it is, 'Tangled Up in Blue.' I can hear that little [guitar riff] and I'll come up to a complete stranger, proud as I am, and say 'That's me.' 'Is that really you?' Some of them believe me, some of them don't. It's a time capsule that just lasts forever. That song is going to be around for a little bit."

As will *Blood on the Tracks*.

Acknowledgments

OUR BOOK BEGAN WITH TRANSCRIPTS OF INTERVIEWS THAT Paul conducted with the musicians for his broadcast show *Wall of Power TV* in 2016–18. All other quotations come from interviews Rick conducted in 2021 with four of the six musicians (Chris Weber and Peter Ostroushko had passed away before we began to write the book) and from the other sources cited in the text.

We wish to thank all the musicians and others whom we interviewed. We also thank Nate Kranz, First Avenue, Marc Percansky, Dave Morton, Hugh Brown, Kelly Hotchkiss, Andy Watson, MCN6, Stuart DeVann, Grumpy's Bar NE, Paul Studahar, Monty Lee Wilkes; Fishman, Disrud, and Fishman Law; Aaron Goodyear, Sean Skinner, Tony Tieberg, Becky Thompson, Jim Tordoff, Vanessa Weber, Nancy Bundt, Bill Pagel, and Herb Pilhofer.

Paul Metsa is a native of Virginia, Minnesota, twenty miles east of Bob Dylan's boyhood home in Hibbing. Winner of eight Minnesota Music Awards, he was called "the other great folk singer from Minnesota's Mesabi Iron Range" by *Huffington Post.* He and Kevin Odegard organized the Million Dollar Bash reunion concert that united most of the Minnesota Six in 2001 to celebrate Dylan's sixtieth birthday. His autobiography *Blue Guitar Highway* was published by the University of Minnesota Press. More information on Paul can be found at www.paulmetsa.com.

Rick Shefchik is a native of Duluth, Minnesota, Bob Dylan's birthplace. He was an award-winning reporter and columnist for the *Duluth News–Tribune* and *St. Paul Pioneer Press* for thirty years. He has written ten books, including *From Fields to Fairways: Classic Golf Clubs of Minnesota* and *Everybody's Heard about the Bird: The True Story of 1960s Rock 'n' Roll in Minnesota,* both published by the University of Minnesota Press. More information on Rick can be found at www.rickshefchik.com.